# THE
# SANTA CLAUS
# PICTURE BOOK

As the first faint stars of the evening begin to appear on the horizon, stately old Père Noël starts on his long Christmas Eve journey. He carries his *cadeaux de fruits* in *une hotte,* the traditional French grape-gathering basket. The various fruits in his pack are old, some made of cotton lint, others of painted velvet. Who knows to whom he will give the red silk rose? French, painted, molded-cardboard Père Noël with grape-gathering basket, H. 21″, c. 1910.

# THE SANTA CLAUS PICTURE BOOK

## AN APPRAISAL GUIDE

## MAGGIE ROGERS
### and
## PETER R. HALLINAN

E.P. DUTTON, INC.
NEW YORK

First published, 1984,
in the United States by E.P. Dutton, Inc., New York.

For information contact: E.P. Dutton, Inc.
2 Park Avenue, New York, N.Y. 10016

Library of Congress Catalog Card Number: 84-71354

Printed and bound by
Dai Nippon Printing Co., Ltd., Tokyo, Japan.
ISBN: 0-525-24282-1 (cloth)
0-525-48148-6 (DP)
Published simultaneously in Canada by
Fitzhenry & Whiteside Limited,
Toronto

Designed by Marilyn Rey

10 9 8 7 6 5 4 3 2 1

First Edition

From Maggie    with love to Aunt, Margaret Jennings,
                    who always encourages me to do my
                    best,
                    says I'm trying to do too much,
                    and then sees me through.

From Peter    to my wife, Jan, one of those
                    who still believes.

# ACKNOWLEDGMENTS

For permitting us to photograph
Christmas figures from their collections, we thank

Frank Adams, Inc.
Barney Barenholtz
Lois Bates
Ginger Burr
Edward Cauduro
Robert Cramer
Glenn and Edith Day
Eric Dehlin
Barbara Eckstrom
Gwyneth Gamble
Judy Hawkins
Bill Hilands
Bertha Hilby
Lynn and Diana Husband
Gertrude Glutsch Jensen
Gladys Lane
Maxine Mallicoat
Giuliano Marcantoni
Gary and Lydell McIlney
Lynetta McKiernan
Robert Merck
Velma Milkowski
Don Millegan
June Nelson
Oliver and Thompson Company
Susan Palmich
Quinland Daniels Porter
Ann Reznick
Marjorie Baker Sawyer
Bob and Barbara Shirk
Susan Shroyer
Allen Simmons
Margaret Soumie

For gracious and generous assistance
in many different ways, we are deeply indebted to

Harry Abrams, Publishers
Karen Arms
Jean Auel
Margaret Benjamin
Heather Bryse-Harvey
Jackie Chamberlain
Ann Davol
Jan Hallinan
Jane Heitkemper
Evadne Ammen Hilands
Gunther and Trudy Hoffmann
Thomas E. B. Jones
Dick and Ruth Keller
Ladies of the Storage Facility, Multnomah County
    Library, Portland, Oregon
Wolfgang and Dawn Merx
Nabisco Corporation
Margaret O'Rourke
David Palmer
Darr Phelps
Bill Potter
Margaret Carhart Powers
Kay Riley
Meg Rogers
Wayne R. Rogers
Travis Simmons
Donald J. Sterling, Jr.
Strohecker's Grocery Store
Townsend Thorndike
Elizabeth Crownhart Vaughan

# CONTENTS

# PREFACE

Our love affair began when I was twelve. My mother, the most imaginative and creative one a child could wish for, had decided I was old enough to have an elegant party. Forty years later, the Christmas tree of that night remains in my memory a shimmery mass of reflected lights. And the table! In the middle of it stood a huge, old-fashioned, white-clad Santa Claus, sparkling with mica dust and wreathed in fresh evergreens. He held red ribbons that led to small individual Santas at each of the twenty places set for my friends. Red carnations and juniper were twined around silver candlesticks and tied with more red ribbons. I still remember the white damask cloth, ironed stiff as a board.

What happened to those Santa decorations I don't remember. That marvelous Santa Claus, however, awoke in me a lifelong love of the ambiance of Christmas, personified so well for young and old alike by old St. Nick. Later, as the mother of three young children, I worked hard to have the most glorious Christmas tree I could create with hundreds of handmade and antique ornaments.

One day a friend gave me an old Father Christmas figure. He was beautiful. White-clad like the one from my childhood, his hood was crowned by a holly wreath studded with red berries. In a rush, the Christmases of my childhood returned. I was irretrievably in love with the old gentleman of Christmas.

My collection of holiday decor shifted from the traditional blown-glass ornaments to these delightful Christmas figures. One thing led to another, and I became a serious student of Christmas. My aunt, who has always nurtured and encouraged in me the love of beauty and the appreciation of the past, picked up on my deepening interest. Said she, at age seventy-nine, "Name one place you'd like to go, and I'll take you there." "Russia," I answered in a breath, and we went! The thing I searched for, of course, was Grandfather Frost—the Russian gift giver, almost impossible to obtain out of season in a country so little dedicated to the whims of the tourist and the ease of the consumer. It was a rough trip for my aunt, but we both exulted, six months after our return home, in the arrival of not one, but two Grandfather Frost figures from Leningrad.

Off on another junket, searching through ten countries and thirteen cities during a European Advent for Father Christmas figures, I discovered just a few of them and, to my surprise and delight, the many joys of photography. Home again, I couldn't wait to get advice from our neighbor, Peter, a professional photographer.

Next thing I knew, we had set out to create a book

that would capture the spirit of the old gift givers. We photographed every Sunday afternoon we could for two years—in the forest, in the photo lab, on Mt. Hood, in old warehouses, and in our basements and backyards.

With the real generosity of Christmas, no one has refused to assist us, whether with knowledge or with the loan of valuable figures. Many have gone far beyond what we hesitantly requested. We extend our thanks and gratitude particularly to Robert Merck for every kind of support he could extend, to Kay Riley of New York City for her continual encouragement, to Karen Arms and Professor Wolfgang and Frau Dawn Merx for translating German sources, which opened up another world. Mere thanks could never repay Evadne Hilands and Meg Rogers for their expert editorial help. Not to be forgotten are the ladies of the Multnomah County Library's Storage Facility who uncomplainingly hauled up from their basement what must have been a ton or more of old books and magazines. They deserve a salute and special thanks. Perhaps most of all, Peter's creativity, optimism, and insistence on getting things just right made our collaboration a constant pleasure. Even now I am sure he is ready to take another picture!

We hope that this book will awaken in others our joy in these personifications of the luscious and colorful warmth, sparkle, and glamour of the Christmas season.

Merry Christmas,
Maggie Rogers

# THE
# SANTA CLAUS
# PICTURE BOOK

# INTRODUCTION

How real the Christmas of our childhood is, still, to most of us. Weeks of anticipation, wild hopes tinged with moments of despair, visions of dolls and bicycles, books and games—and candy. Imagined sounds of reindeer hoofs on the roof Christmas Eve, the sleepless, fitful night. But next morning! How could we ever forget the grand climax next morning! Full stockings and the tree heavy-laden with mysterious, lumpy packages. Hurrah! Hurrah! Santa has come again!

This is a book about the gift givers of Christmas. We in America call our favorite gift giver Santa Claus: a jolly, generous, loving fellow who knows our innermost desires, and who, if we have kept our part of the bargain, rewards us well from his ample pack. We would recognize him anywhere with his curly whiskers, his furry, scarlet coat, and his baggy trousers. Yet how many of us realize that he is the almost direct descendant of St. Nicholas, a fourth-century bishop of the early Christian Church, whose outlines have blurred over the past sixteen hundred years?

St. Nicholas, Bishop of Myra in Asia Minor during the fourth century A.D., became the first gift giving personality of the yuletide feast. Already known and revered throughout Europe for his good deeds and miracles, his fame steadily increased after his death in A.D. 343. Although little historical evidence is available to us, the day of his death, December 6, has always been kept as St. Nicholas's Day. Seated on his white horse, resplendent in colorful embroidered robes and miter, carrying his golden crozier, his image fired people's imaginations. The Russians adopted him as their protector, and as word about him traveled northward, he became the trusted saint of both Lapps and Samoyeds. Over the centuries myriad legends have grown up around him. Children, merchants, sailors, bankers, even pawnbrokers and thieves have come to name him their patron saint. A beloved cosmopolitan figure, no other saint in the ecclesiastical calendar can claim such fealty.

No central gift giving figure had emerged until the appearance of St. Nicholas, although gift giving had been a ritual since earliest pagan days. Before the advent of Christianity, winter festivals were held in Rome, in the Teutonic and Celtic areas of northern and western Europe, and in Asia Minor and Persia to celebrate the yearly rebirth of the sun after it had reached its lowest point in the cold, gray sky. These bacchanals were characterized by wild drinking and feasting, gambling, singing, and exchanges of small gifts, such as terra-cotta dolls and little wax tapers to symbolize the renascence of life.

During the early Christian era that followed, waning pagan beliefs and rituals began to be assimilated

1

into Christian practices. Nonetheless, many pagan customs, although transformed, remain today as cherished parts of our present-day Christmas. It is easy to understand how the idea of gift giving, first found in pagan celebrations, was maintained, even heightened, by the legends of the genial and generous old Bishop of Myra.

During the Middle Ages Christmas was celebrated with an unspoken truce between church and laity. General carousing coexisted with the annual celebration of Christ's birth. Moralistic mystery plays competed with the more popular juggling and mummery. By the fourteenth century, kings and nobles undertook Christmas entertaining on a vast scale. The Colleges and Inns of Court in England joined in the revels. Royal treasuries were strained to meet the expenses of Christmas. Huge amounts of money were expended for gold cloth, jeweled drinking beakers, and costly gifts to noblemen.

A no-account poet of Victorian times, a Mr. Whistlecraft, is responsible for this enumeration of good eats supposedly served up at King Arthur's table on Christmas Day:

> They served up salmon, venison, and wild boars,
> By hundreds, and by dozens, and by scores.
> Hogsheads of honey, kilderkins of mustard,
> Muttons, and batted beeves, and bacon swine;
> Herons and bitterns, peacocks, swan, and bustard,
> Teal, mallard, pigeons, widgeons, and in fine,
> Plum-puddings, pancakes, apple-pies, and custard.
> And therewithal they drank good Gascon wine,
> With mead, and ale, and cider of our own;
> For porter, punch, and negus were not known.

All this excess was to change. In the sixteenth century, when the Protestant Reformation, led by Martin Luther, made it unpopular to celebrate any occasion connected with a saint, St. Nicholas merely changed his name to Father Christmas in England, *Weihnachtsmann*, "the Christmas man," in Germany, and Père Noël in France.

The Englishman Ben Jonson, in his *Masque of Christmas*, written in 1616, describes the English Father Christmas in detail, referring to him as "Christmas, Old Christmas, Christmas of London, and Captain Christmas." The old gentleman is introduced "attired in round hose, long stockings, a close doublet, a high-crowned hat, with a broach, a long, thin beard, a truncheon, little ruffs, white shoes, his scarfs and garters tied cross and his drum beaten before him." Both the Protestant and Catholic Netherlands, however, retained December 6 as St. Nicholas Day, but the Protestants changed the day from a

religious to a secular one, and the old saint took on the attributes of Father Christmas and Père Noël.

The split with Rome also dimmed the joyous Christmas of the past in England, as the Long Parliament with Cromwell as a member, in 1642, closed the churches and opened stores and markets for business on Christmas Day. But the celebration could not be extinguished entirely, and it went underground. Christmas was more privately kept in a gentler fashion until 1660, when Charles II returned to the throne and ordered the resumption of the public holiday. Unfortunately, the Puritans had outlawed Christmas for too long—eighteen years—long enough for many of the old customs to disappear. And so the holiday was quietly observed with no special fanfare until its tremendous resurgence in the nineteenth century, ushered in on a wave of new romantic feeling.

Father Christmas evolved as the spirit of Christmas with origins from both St. Nicholas and pagan predecessors. He was a two-sided personality coming both to reward and to punish: part Saturn, the god who brought food and drink and revelry to the Roman Saturnalia, and part Thor, the Norse god of war who, when angered, roared through the heavens in his goat-drawn chariot, which crashed lightning and thunder in his path. Thor lived among the Northern people and was constantly battling the gods of ice and snow as he attempted to ease the miseries of winter for his people. Thor was sometimes represented as an old man with a long white beard.

Father Christmas appeared often in illustrations during the nineteenth century, wearing great fur robes, crowned with wreaths of holly, ivy, or mistletoe, carrying a yule log or bowl of Christmas punch. More frequently he is seen with his hands clenched around switches, ready to punish recalcitrant children, yet lugging a huge sack of toys on his back. He never assumes the rotundity of Santa Claus or his joyous mien, and he eventually faded from view as Santa's heart captured the world.

Germany established the Christ Child as gift giver after the demise of St. Nicholas. The *Christkind* would eventually be corrupted to Kris Kringle as the Germans settled in the Pennsylvania German area of the United States. But the Dutch, who had retained St. Nicholas, brought St. Nicholas with them when they settled New Amsterdam (later to become New York City). Over the years, in the vernacular of the day, St. Nicholas began to be pronounced *Sinter Claes*, just a slip away from Santa Claus.

Sinter Claes stayed with the Dutch until after the American Revolution in 1776, because America had Puritan beginnings that rejected both Catholic saints and Christmas celebrations. It was actually illegal to observe the holiday in any way throughout the four New England colonies: Connecticut, Massachusetts Bay, Plymouth, and New Haven. After the war, however, the Christmas customs of the Dutch gradually began to seep into the general population. And a book written by a member of the Dutch community caught the imagination of the American public. St. Nicholas was at last in the public eye of the New World.

Washington Irving's satirical best seller, written in 1809, *Diedrich Knickerbocker's A History of New York from the Beginning of the World to the End of the Dutch Dynasty*, stayed in print for over twenty years. The book introduced St. Nicholas as the patron saint of the Dutch and described how the saint rode over housetops "drawing forth magnificent presents and dropping them down the chimneys of his favorites." In later pages, Irving elaborated a little more on just what St. Nicholas did. He wrote, "Now he visits us but one night in the year when he rattles down the chimneys . . . confining his presents merely to children." "Stockings," he added, "[are] found in the morning mysteriously filled." Irving is responsible, too, for the changes in the episcopal robes that were replaced by a typical Dutch costume: a low, broadbrimmed hat, a long pair of trunk hose, and a large pipe. One last Irving passage pictured the old saint as a jolly elf, skyward-bound, with a pack on his back, distributing gifts from a horse-drawn wagon.

Irving was the first of three Americans credited with the creation of the American Santa Claus, who evolved over a period of eighty years. The second was a young professor at a theological seminary, Dr. Clement Clarke Moore. The father of six, Moore often composed works for family events. In 1823 he dashed off "A Visit from St. Nicholas" for just such an occasion. Moore must have been acquainted with a slim little volume that had been published two years before by an unknown author, *A New Year's Present to the Little Ones from Five to Twelve*, the first book about Christmas printed in America, the first to picture St. Nicholas sitting in a sleigh pulled by a reindeer, and the first to feature hanging stockings at Christmastime to hold gifts. Reverend Moore increased the number of reindeer to eight and added merriment by giving each animal a stylish name. He lifted one passage that sounds suspiciously like Irving.

Irving wrote in his best seller:

Laying his finger beside his nose, [he] gave a very significant look, then mounting his wagon, he returned over the tree tops and disappeared.

Moore's poem reads:

[He] fill'd all the stockings: then turned with a jerk,
and laying his finger aside of his nose,
and giving a nod, up the chimney he rose. . . .

Moore softens Irving's somewhat ascetic, but nonetheless jolly elf into a round and rosy old elf:

He was dressed all in fur, from his head to his foot,
And his clothes were all tarnished with ashes and soot;
A bundle of toys he had flung on his back,
And he looked like a pedlar just opening his pack.
His eyes—how they twinkled! his dimples how merry!
His cheeks were like roses, his nose like a cherry!
His droll little mouth was drawn up like a bow,
And the beard of his chin was as white as the snow;
The stump of a pipe he held tight in his teeth,
And the smoke it encircled his head like a wreath,
He had a broad face, and a round little belly
That shook, when he laughed, like a bowl full of jelly.
He was chubby and plump, a right jolly old elf,
And I laughed when I saw him, in spite of myself. . . .

By the 1860s Santa Claus had become a household world. The old mispronounced Sinter Claes eventually slipped into the widely accepted Santa Claus. But though most people knew of him by name, few had a clear picture of him. In one magazine illustration of the day, he appeared clad in buckskin; in another, he wore a carpenter's apron.

The great American political cartoonist Thomas Nast, a Santa buff himself, must have realized that "one picture is worth a thousand words," and he set out to remedy the situation. He used himself as the model for his drawings. In 1862 he drew his first Santa sketch for *Harper's Weekly Magazine*. *Harper's* published over thirty Nast Santa cartoons over the next twenty-two years. He copied the fur suits of Bavarian Father Christmas figures he had seen as a child. The Nast Santa was a jolly, plump, gnomelike character with an infectious outgoing personality. He often carried a long telescope and a record book, useful tools in his kind of work. Nast did a final series of colored cartoons for the publishers, McLoughlin Brothers. In them Santa was bedecked in a bright red suit trimmed in white ermine. Otherwise the illustrations in *Santa Claus and His Works*, published in the late 1880s, were black-and-white drawings.

There were no significant changes in Santa lore for seventy-five years. In the 1930s Santa's features grew coarser as he became rounder. The Coca-Cola Company portrayed him in their ads as an even more

1. The stark facial features and overall fragility of this primitive Father Christmas impart a sense of nostalgia for Christmases long, long ago. A collector's dream, this mechanical figure not only moves but also plays music. When the handle in the base is turned, the puppet-on-a-string flails its arms up and down, and the music box pings out a haunting, unidentifiable melody. German, mechanical Father Christmas, papier-mâché face, rabbit-fur beard, wood hands and boots, goose-feather tree, cotton-lint and composition fruit, H. 8″, lithographed tin music box, H. 5¼″, 1890–1900.

human character. For the first time, he had blue eyes, ruby red lips, and a ruddy complexion. Some critics believe that the simple mystique of the Nast Santa is more appealing than the fleshed-out Coca-Cola figure, but they are in the minority. The new Santa Claus took America by storm—they loved him and do to this day! His new features were quickly accepted and used in magazines, stationery products, store displays, Christmas decorations, and confectionery.

Although Santa Claus has changed superficially in appearance from austere Father Christmas to jolly St. Nick, in essence the spirit of the gift giver has changed little from that of the Bishop of Myra who inspired him so long ago. However, it was the period of Irving, Moore, and Nast that saw the progression from word pictures to drawings and other illustrations to freestanding Father Christmas figures. They have been produced in every decade since the late nineteenth century. Curiously enough, it was the Victorians, undergoing a period of nostalgia similar to the one in America during the 1960s, who first produced them. The celebration of Christmas had never completely recovered from the time of its suppression in England from 1642 to 1660. Even after the monarchy had been restored and the holiday reinstated, the yuletide festival remained subdued. Victorians here and abroad hungered for the Christmas of olden days, and the times were right for it to reemerge in all its former glory: the age saw the flowering of the Industrial Revolution and the flagrant materialism it fostered. The rich became richer and the poor, poorer. But almost as a contradiction, the age also witnessed a great wave of religious fervor that stressed charity toward one's neighbor. Thus evolved a citizenry who were overly generous, overly indulgent, and overly sentimental. Children were sweet and were often portrayed with cloying sweetness; Christmas was marked by excess everywhere—in gift giving, in decorations, in food.

As the century progressed and consumer goods came within the reach of the populace, more people could enjoy the lush trappings of a good Christmas. Christmas cards came into existence; turkeys and crackers became popular. Money was lavished in increasing amounts on holiday decorating. The Christmas tree, a custom imported from Germany, became widely accepted.

As one motto of the modern world might be "Less is more," the Victorians, by contrast, embraced the concept of "More is best"! They loved clutter, and lots of it. They possessed amazingly inventive minds that manifested themselves in intricate, romantic creations of careful craftsmanship and charm. The colors they used were at once both bright and soft. Their works often evoke immediate emotional responses, so direct is their appeal. Such were many of the Father Christmas figures made during these years.

Most of the early Christmas figures from this Victorian period are made of papier mâché and are the prizes of serious collectors. Papier mâché is a combination of pulp paper, glue or paste, oil, and rosin or other sizing. Using a *Drucken,* the mixture is pressed into two half-molds. After the two forms have dried in the molds, they are removed, glued together, and put aside. Later the seams are smoothed with fine sandpaper, sealed with varnish, and painted, usually white, but sometimes in a color. Detailing on the faces of the Victorian figures was painstaking; no two faces were alike and they showed highly individualistic styling. Germans typically painted eyes with "dot" pupils surrounded by little colored dabs of iris, black lid lining, and one-stroke brows in reddish-brown. Often they would finish by applying a single dot of red to the inner corner of the upper lid. Occasionally red lines appeared on foreheads and around eyes to portray more fearsome countenances.

Although the art of making papier-mâché figures goes back to the eighteenth century, most were made after 1890 around Sonneberg in present-day East Germany, the doll center of the world at that time. Seventy-five percent of the work was done in the homes, and at its peak, the Sonneberg cottage industry employed 30,000 people. Wages were appallingly low, and most of the papier-mâché products, which included "Nicholas" men, Christmas ornaments, Easter eggs, hens, and rabbits, were made for export.

Even more difficult to find today than the simple papier-mâché Father Christmas figures are the Pelze-Nicol forms with the genuine fur coats. When St. Nicholas was replaced by the Christ Child during the 1600s in northern Germany, he was demoted to the lowly Pelze-Nicol, the frightful "fur-coated Nicholas" who accompanied the Christ Child and knew everyone's sins. Often called Belsnickles today, which phonetically closely approximates Pelze-Nicols, these figures are extremely hard to find, as the Germans made far fewer of them than *Weihnachtsmänner,* the old Christmas men of southern Germany.

Another scarce form of papier-mâché that exists today, some people call *composition.* It has roots in the 1800s, when the Germans made papier-mâché dolls and doll heads that were dipped into liquid plaster. The plaster dried in a very thin coat, which left an ultrasmooth surface on which to paint fine details. Paint flowed particularly well on such a sur-

2. Hand-carved wooden arms and legs give an indication of the early manufacture of this grim and forbidding Father Christmas. Even his suit is unfinished, adding to the wonderful primitive feeling of the piece. He is leaning against a large goose-feather tree. German, Father Christmas, composition face, rabbit-fur beard and hair, wooden arms, legs, and feet, wool suit and cap, H. 6″, early 1890s.

face, and the colors have an unusual richness. The Germans used this technique on a group of Father Christmas figures that have very ruddy complexions. Many of the figures in this category stand in stooped postures and often wear velvet suits, which over the years have faded to a lovely tomato-soup color. Care must be taken when handling these figures: the bond between the papier-mâché and the plaster is not strong, and the plaster chips easily.

Favorites of German children as well as of many collectors today are the cotton-wadding or -batting figures of Father Christmas that were produced in the small town of Lauscha, near Sonneberg, in present-day East Germany. While Lauscha's major interest was in producing blown-glass Christmas ornaments, its other main concern was its cottage cotton industry, making both artificial flowers and Christmas ornaments from cotton. Cotton-wadding figures had first been crafted in Norway, then in Austria, and finally in Germany in the second half of the nineteenth century. Norwegians had traditionally pulled cotton apart, spreading it on tree branches to resemble snow. They liked its appearance so much that they began making cotton figures for their trees. A small number of German figures were also made in Frankfurt until 1908. One Christmas catalogue featured a wide selection of wonderful, fanciful objects: a chapel with a gold angel on top, a rooster with a real

feather tail, a muff with flowers, and, of course, a white-coated Nicholas man, to mention a few.

The figures were relatively easy to make. People worked in their homes, sometimes using wrapping machines for decorations like icicles, snowballs, mushrooms, and the figures' arms and legs. For one-dimensional figures, the cotton was merely cut in layers, rolled, and then glued together. For sparkle, mica dust was glued on wherever needed. "Scrap" faces, hands, and feet were added, and then came the final embellishments: flowers, ribbons, tinsel, *Erika-moos* (dried, dyed bog heather indigenous to Europe, southern Scandinavia, Britain, and Spain), gold wings, crepe-paper skirts and aprons, leaves, gold paper or tinsel buttons, and, on some figures, cardboard skis.

Cotton-wadding figures are relatively hard to find, as German children were sometimes allowed to play with them at times other than Christmas. They disintegrated easily with hard play, and a figure in pristine condition is a great find. These figures evoke real feelings of nostalgia. They are surpassed by few old Christmas decorations and are much in demand.

Scrap, used on many Christmas men, was called *Glanzbilder* by the Germans in the 1890s. These colored, embossed pictures were made possible by a new printing process that had emerged in 1830. Chromolithography reached the zenith of its popularity at the turn of the century, and scrap appeared on a wide variety of Christmas figures. Often Victorian children filled scrapbooks with collections of these colored pictures, hence the derivation of the word *scrapbook*.

The Germans liked to embellish their creations, in true Victorian fashion, with tinsel and *Erikamoos* to give them a lively holiday look. Tinsel had first been used on French military uniforms; *Erikamoos* proved an effective, long-lasting substitute for greenery. It is still available today.

Especially beautiful Father Christmas figures from this same period are those made of spun glass. The process involved in making spun glass sounds difficult, but with continued practice German spinners quickly became accomplished. One worker stood in front of the spinner, holding a glass rod in a hot flame. He touched the rod to another heated glass rod, over the flame, and quickly pulled the two apart, drawing out a thin glass filament. The spinner caught the filament on a big wheel, five feet in diameter, and kept it rotating at a steady speed. Afterward, the thread was wound onto bobbins to be used in various ways at a later time. Most spun glass was fabricated for industrial purposes; however, in Lauscha it was used exclusively for decorations. Wrapping machines wound figures of spun glass in much the same way that cotton figures were made. The machines shaped simple forms like snowmen, icicles, doll pillows, and Nicholas men. Later, Germans discovered that spun glass could be curled. Called "elves' hair," it was used for Father Christmas beards and as snow on tree branches.

The German makers were fond of combining materials; they might put a wax head on a spun-glass Father Christmas body, for example. All-wax figures were rare except for Christ Child and angel forms. To make a hollow wax head, a worker poured melted wax at just the correct temperature into a mold, waited a few moments, and then poured the excess out. He then repeated the process so that several layers would be built up. This technique increased the strength of the form and prevented it from sinking inward as it cooled. The wax head was then painted carefully to achieve the desired facial expression. At other times, the workers applied scrap to finish a Christmas figure. This was simply glued onto the spun glass along with other trimmings.

As mentioned before, Lauscha was best known for its lovely glass ornaments. That industry got under way in the 1880s, and by the 1890s many pieces had started to arrive in America. As soon as Americans saw the ornaments, they clamored for more.

By 1910 thousands were being sold each Christmas. Thuringian glassmakers blew Father Christmas and Santa Claus figures into plaster molds. After the forms had cooled, they were removed from the molds, silvered inside, lacquered outside, trimmed, and hand-decorated. Lauschan children then capped the ornaments and packed them for export. These ornaments were paper-thin, light, and extremely fragile. The oldest ones are delicately molded and show off the subtle Victorian coloring to the best advantage. The rarest of these feature Father Christmas and Santa figures flying in an airplane, sitting atop a zodiac crystal ball, or riding on a horse. Another scarce ornament is a full-bodied glass Santa with chenille legs and composition boots. Early glass figures command good prices, especially the out-of-the-ordinary Santa ornaments.

Some Christmas figures were composed of plaster or chalk, notably crèche pieces. But the *Weihnachtsmann* figure in these media is not so common as that of other materials. Some of them are merely freestanding statues, whereas others are meant to hold candy. A plaster Christmas light in the shape of a Father Christmas head is a very rare form. These lights were made between 1890 and 1910. They are heavy, but nevertheless are meant to hang on tree limbs. Coupled with the candle that was placed inside, they must have weighed the limb down considerably! Plaster figures were formed in wooden molds, then painted and trimmed.

Many wooden and Celluloid Christmas men were also available as decorations, either to hang on trees or to be freestanding. The wooden ones were undoubtedly the most desirable, as parents preferred less-breakable decorations. Basically toys, the wooden *Weihnachtsmänner* came from the Erzgebirge and Berchtesgaden mountain areas of Germany, as many still do today. Included in this group of wooden figures are also the "smokers" and nutcrackers, first made in Santa form thirty years ago from a design by Olga Whitehurst, an American importer. These are manufactured in both the Erzgebirge and Olbernhau regions of East Germany today. Similar figures are also being produced in Lauingen, a small village in West Germany near Augsburg. Santas of this kind are available in many sizes, some extremely tall; they are brightly colored and eye-catching. Children love them. So do many adults who collect them. All were carefully worked, sanded, and painted. Some examples of fine old workmanship have managed to survive. Today, sad to say, the quality of German craftsmanship is beginning to slip: an occasional piece turns up roughly sanded and painted in a slapdash manner.

The first Celluloid items appeared in 1869. It was

3. The goats of Thor must have inspired the Althof, Bergmann Company of New York to fashion this extremely rare Santa-in-a-sleigh pulled by goats. Founded in 1856, the reputable old firm imported toys and china. But more important, it manufactured horse-drawn vehicles of all types, novelty toys, floor trains, and boats. When this toy is wound, the wheels begin to move, and the goats go up and down. A special attachment on the rear legs of the goats causes the bells to jingle. Only a few toys like this are known to exist. American, Santa, composition face, wood body, crepe-paper suit with fur trim, fur mittens. Sleigh: chromolithographed tin, metal bells, ribbon reins; clockwork mechanism, 9″ x 18″, late 1800s. (Photo courtesy Harry Abrams, Inc., from *American Antique Toys*, 1980, by Bernard Barenholtz and Inez McClintock; photo by Bill Holland)

not until around 1875 that mold makers in Mannheim, Germany, perfected the process enough to turn out Christmas figures, toys, and dolls. Twenty years later, the well-known Lenel Bensinger Company of Mannheim was stamping its products with the familiar turtle mark that has always represented quality. Celluloid can be molded in minute detail and used in a dilute form to paint the figures. It is possible to achieve lovely coloring on Celluloid. However, such figures have many disadvantages: they are flammable, are easily dented, and they yellow with age. Because of their flammability many were lost forever in tree fires. Although collectors naturally prefer papier-mâché and cotton figures to Celluloid ones, a Celluloid Nicholas man with good molding and color is still an excellent find. Some of the faces on the Celluloid pieces seem almost alive.

Besides papier-mâché, plaster, spun glass, blown glass, wood, and Celluloid, some Christmas figures were made from metal: cast iron, lead, and tin. Cast-iron Santas appeared as an integral part of banks, both mechanical and still, which were, surprisingly enough, not German-made, but American! The best-quality banks were produced between 1860 and 1930. Although rarity is a factor in appraising a bank, other considerations include its general appeal, over-

all workmanship, country of origin (tin banks are German), and the demand for the item. Santa banks are both rare and nostalgic, and value escalates as both Christmas collectors and bank collectors seek them out.

Lead Christmas figures were never as much in demand as lead soldiers. Made after 1850 in steel molds, lead Father Christmas and Santa figures can best be dated by the style of their clothing and general body conformation.

Antique tin Father Christmas items are also rare and beautiful. Amazingly enough, tin toys originated in the United States, not in Germany. In Europe the industry got off to a much slower start. The Industrial Revolution, which gave rise to Christmas cards and decorations, also promoted the production of tin toys. It provided the skilled labor, the factories, and the new machines to make them. For the first time thin-sheet steel could be bonded to tin. Superbly finished, the toys were decorated either by chromolithography, before the metal was pressed, or by hand-painting after the metal parts were assembled. Sections of toys were either soldered or joined with bent metal tabs. Production rose rapidly in the 1890s, and the quality of toys reached its zenith at this time. The consensus among collectors is that American tin toys were always more imaginative and fanciful than the more ponderous German models.

At the turn of the century Father Christmas decorations could be purchased from toy and novelty stores, catalogues, and holiday exhibitions and trade fairs. A noticeable increase in the advertising of Christmas toys and novelties began in the 1870s. One firm, Horsman, Strasberger, and Pfeiffer in New York, featured foreign imports, and the Althof, Bergmann Company offered "elegant toys and fancy goods." F.A.O. Schwarz held "Grand Holiday Exhibitions," advertising "The Latest and Rarest Novelties in Toys, Dolls, Games, and Fancy Goods." All three of these firms kept extended hours during December, with Santa Claus headquarters in a prime store location. B. Shackman, Inc., on lower Fifth Avenue in Manhattan today, was a pioneer toy and novelty firm. The founder, Bertha Shackman, opened the family business in 1898.

A beloved American institution was established in 1879. F. W. Woolworth, president of the five-and-dime-store chain bearing his name, made many trips to Lauscha to purchase Christmas decorations over the years. He alone is responsible for millions of those that were sold in the United States as he imported them to feature in his variety stores throughout the nation.

The end of the nineteenth century also saw the rise of mail-order catalogues from other chain stores like Montgomery Ward and Sears, Roebuck. Their catalogues always had pages devoted to the newest toys and Christmas favors and decorations. What child could forget poring over the "Wish Book" from the minute it arrived until the great day itself? Decorations in the catalogues were reasonably priced; this included the Father Christmas and Santa Claus figures. Without doubt, many of those we cherish today came from these stores.

Macy's department store distributed its first toy catalogue in 1885. Various other toy stores in New York had catalogues in the late 1800s. The Erlich Brothers and the Amos M. Lyon Company were wholesalers and importers of toys, Christmas ornaments, and decorations. Both offered a wide selection of cotton-wadding figures.

Another factor influenced the sale of Christmas figures, in addition to advertising and mail-order catalogues. International trade exhibitions, held in Paris, London, New York, Philadelphia, and Chicago, whetted the public's appetite for foreign goods. Toys, dolls, and novelties were all part of the nineteenth-century exhibitions. Many were purchased abroad as people learned about what they had seen. It must also be remembered that the largest wave of German immigrants arrived in America in the 1880s—a number that has never been exceeded either before or since. Even second- and third-generation Americans continued to hold dear their Old World heritage, particularly at Christmas, and if their elders had not brought a touch of old Christmas with them, they sent to their homeland for it.

Often Christmas novelties and decorations so dear to Victorian hearts were designed to hold holiday sweets. No Victorian would dream of celebrating a festive day without sweets! Many Father Christmas and Santa figures have hidden cylinders within them for just this purpose. Some Santa figures stood perched on boxes that were designed to contain small trinkets, money, or even ice cream. Many ladies' household magazines gave instructions on how to line the boxes in order to make them both sanitary and liquid-proof! These "bonbonières" were common features in many old-time periodicals, with directions given on how to construct simple candy containers at home.

At the beginning of the nineteenth century most candy was homemade. Favorite Christmas sweets included maple panocha, peppermint drops, nut crackle, walnut molasses, and the old stand-by, vinegar taffy. While candy and candy recipes were featured in ladies' magazines, articles also appeared warning against overindulgence in sweets by the young, predicting dire consequences unless moderation was observed.

Although there were only a few hundred candy manufacturers in the United States in 1850, there were some 1,314 in 1935. Candy was not consumed moderately, and at Christmastime people felt particularly free to indulge. Over the years Father Christmas and Santa Claus continued to hide candy, not only in boxes but also in little bags slung over their shoulders.

And what Victorian Christmas would have been complete without a chocolate Father Christmas to munch on? (But, oh, the agony of eating his head!) The Germans made very detailed chocolate molds, in varying sizes, of St. Nicholas, Father Christmas, and later, Santa Claus. In making the chocolate figures, they found they could not simply pour melted chocolate into the molds and turn out perfect forms. They first had to temper the chocolate. *Tempered* chocolate is melted chocolate that registers between 85 degrees and 88 degrees on a candy thermometer. This they poured into two tin half-molds held together at the sides with strong metal clips. If the molds were not completely dry, the chocolate would mold imperfectly. A hollow figure was fashioned by rotating the mold to coat the sides evenly. Allowed to cool for about a half-hour, the figure was unmolded in a room at 50 degrees and left there until completely hardened.

Of course, there were other dainties! Baked goods,

*back formen,* were hanging on European Christmas trees long before they were brought to America in the nineteenth century. The Germans and the Swiss made cookies in wooden molds, which included *Springerle, Tirggel, Printen,* and *Eierzucken.* The old molds, finely carved in soft fruitwood, are now so highly prized that they hang on German kitchen walls as decoration throughout the year. Most of the molded cookies have a cameo surface that browns lightly in the oven; at one time, the cookies were painted with vegetable dyes to use as decorations. Molds had interesting motifs: Nicholas men, rococo ladies, elegant horsemen, Adam and Eve, even Nativity figures.

Later in the nineteenth century, painting cookies was replaced by outlining them with frosting. Then some unknown German invented the cookie cutter! Housewives were delighted by the tin cookie cutters, peddled by itinerant tinsmiths. It was a source of great pride to own an exclusive cutter, especially when the number and variety of cutters seemed unlimited. Cookie cutters in the shape of Father Christmas and Santa Claus are very common; the older ones can easily be identified because they are made of heavier metal and have more complicated outlines. Some have shallow little pieces soldered onto the form to allow greater detail to be pressed into the cookie dough. Because nineteenth-century cookie dough was thicker and denser, it undoubtedly required a stronger metal cutter to cut through it.

Christmas is synonymous with feasting, and the holiday table setting is one of the joys of the celebration. Almost from the moment of their inception around 1890, papier-mâché Father Christmas and Santa Claus figures were incorporated into table decorations, either as centerpieces or as individual favors. This was particularly true of children's tables. Household magazines offered scores of ideas for novel table settings, combining figures with evergreens, garlands of tinsel and popcorn, holly, bayberry candles, ribbons, cotton snowballs, sleighs and reindeer, poinsettias and cyclamens, mirrors, and on and on. A December issue of one of these magazines, after the turn-of-the century, pictured a spectacular table setting for a child's holiday party that incorporated three different Santas into one centerpiece! The first Santa was flying in an airship suspended from the chandelier; the second sat in a sleigh on the roof of a little cottage in the center of the table; and the third Santa was riding in a ship supported on the imaginary waters of its mirrored base, close to the cottage. Consider for a moment the effort of that mother, who concocted such an elaborate party decoration for her children. Using Christmas figures on

tables continued to be in vogue until the 1930s; although they have been in use since then, other decorating schemes have become more fashionable.

Around 1910 another kind of Father Christmas candy holder appeared. This one had a smooth, porcelainlike finish. Made of a mix of plaster of paris, sawdust, and sometimes glue, it was termed *molded cardboard.* The combination was poured into half-molds and allowed to dry; later the two halves were glued together and painted. The claylike surface took paint exceptionally well, resulting in deep brilliant colors. The figures were lightweight. Many of the Christmas men of this type are pictured on holiday tables seen in the *Ladies' Home Journal, Woman's Home Companion, The Delineator,* and *Good Housekeeping* magazines of this decade.

World War I brought immense changes to the world of dolls, toys, and Christmas decorations. The United States placed an embargo on all German imports in 1914, and Japan, for the first time, stepped in to fill the breach. The Golden Age of Christmas figures (1890–1920) was over, even though the Germans produced many fine figures after the war.

One area in which the Germans retained their superiority was the doll trade. Their new bisque dolls, introduced in the 1920s, were tremendous commercial successes: the Kewpies, the Bye-los of Grace Storey Putnam, the Flappers, and the "Immobile Teenies." All these dolls shared a tradition of superb dollmaking around 1870 in Thuringia, Germany. The "Immobile Teenies" were teeny and were made of white bisque. Many of the tiny dolls lacked color because they were not glazed. Perhaps the nature of the subject seemed to demand color, because most of the Santa "Teenies" are highly decorated. Although labeled "immobile," the Santas are frequently involved with cars, wheelbarrows, perambulators, motorcycles—-things that move!

Bisque heads were sometimes combined with other materials to form Father Christmas and Santa figures, as were wax heads, by both the Germans and the Japanese. German bisque, in dolls, figurines, and other fine objets d'art, remains unsurpassed in the world. Japanese bisque is much inferior—rough, ill-trimmed, poorly colored, and badly painted, for the most part. Frequently, doll parts, like arms and legs, do not match. Of course, there are exceptions to the rule, and some fine bisque pieces were created by Japanese artisans.

To make bisque figures, liquid clay, together with feldspar as a fluxing agent, was poured into a plaster mold. The plaster absorbed the water, and the clay set up, becoming greenware. When "leather hard,"

10

4. Although the bisque face on this Father Christmas resembles those of contemporary Taiwan, he is really an old German figure found in an attic where he remained untouched for decades. As a matter of fact, the entire figure is strange. A bevy of Kestner dolls in the background completes this scene of a Christmas of yesteryear. German, bisque-faced Father Christmas, arms, legs, and pack of painted wound paper, crepe-paper cap, wax paper over layered tissue robe, candy container log of *faux* bark, H. 5″, c. 1890.

the greenware was trimmed, marked, incised if necessary, and then thoroughly dried. It was meticulously finished by sanding and finally was fired in a kiln. The degree to which it was finished determined the excellence of a piece. There is a slight drag to old pieces that is not found on the newer ones.

After World War I Japan became the largest exporter of toys and novelties in the international marketplace. Originally made in homes as a cottage industry, Japanese factories took over the manufacture of many of them in the late 1920s as the country underwent a tremendous trade expansion. Emphasis was placed on quantity, not quality. A book written in 1934, *The Secret of Japanese Commercial Expansion*, provided some insight into how this was accomplished so well and so rapidly. Chapter 4 describes the Japanese worker as "industrious, competitive, studious, dexterous, and loves nature." In later pages the book tells how the Japanese government provided for its workers housed in government dormitories and how it organized their physical culture, medical attention, after-hours education, and recreational clubs. The book discussed motivational pay, rest days, the improvement of factory equipment, the elimination of factory waste, the importance of

family honor, and love of country. The plan paid off. The United States in particular saw a wave of Japanese goods pouring into the country during the 1920s and 1930s.

Japan, it must be remembered, was never, and is not now, a Christian country, even though Christianity was introduced into Japan by St. Francis Xavier in 1549. Missionary work commenced under modern conditions after the Restoration of Emperor Mutsuhito in 1868, but the Japanese observed Christmas without any real Christian beliefs. The idea of Father Christmas, spread largely by the cinema and newspapers, quickly caught on with Japanese children. Their clamor for all the festivities that surround him was so persuasive that their parents relented and accepted the old man into their hearts as well. Children were positive that he would visit them, not coming down their chimneys but through their *shoji*, or sliding doors. Many Japanese families would never be affluent enough for an elaborate holiday feast, and most had never even seen a live turkey except perhaps in a zoo. Yet they managed to supply enough sweets for their children to signal the specialness of Christmas Day. Like children the world around, the Japanese soon recognized the white-bearded, kindly gentleman bearing his bag of treats, and there was hardly a home in Japan where he was not warmly welcomed.

Thus it is no wonder that a flood of inexpensive Japanese Santa Claus figures should overtake the American market. Always cheap, they nonetheless possess so much whimsy that they will never be considered second-rate. Even today they are becoming hard to find. The salient feature of the Japanese Santa has to be the typical clay face, which is always rough. Oddly enough, it does not detract from their appeal, but heightens it. Japanese Santas always sport cotton beards, and although they may wear robes of cotton wadding, flannel, or crepe paper, the use of chenille or pipe cleaners, maribou, and foil or paper as trim is a giveaway to their nationality. Then too, Japanese Santas carry bottle-brush trees. This contrasts with the German figures, which always carry trees made of dyed goose feathers.

Candy containers, copied from German prototypes, were made by Japanese workers; however, the Japanese went a step further and made Santa candy bags of netting material, using either clay or Celluloid for the faces, hands, and feet. (Early on, the Germans had fashioned paper or metal cornucopias for candy with scrap Santa faces as trim, something the Japanese never thought to duplicate.)

The Japanese showed great ingenuity in their Christmas decorations. Especially interesting are the large numbers of "hanging" Santas—Santa incorporated into a bell, Santa as a part of a boot, Santa in a chenille shoe. Another collectible field features Santa Claus as an integral part of a cottage or church scene. But most fun are the Santas with the wild and raw Japanese coloring: the pinks, greens, and blues seen on so many cheap novelty wares. They are wonderful! It is debatable whether the good old Bishop of Myra would have admitted to being related to these garish Japanese fellows!

The Japanese liked the German Santas-in-the-sleigh and copied them, too. Sent by the thousands to the United States, they proved to be extremely popular with Americans. Japanese sleighs were usually fabricated of cardboard; the Germans preferred to use wood whenever possible. The Japanese reindeer were Celluloid as were so many of the novelties they exported during these years. Some reindeer were pink, some red, others brown, still others white. Most had painted eyes, but at times the reindeer's eyes were bejeweled with pink or deep blue rhinestones. The Germans, on the other hand, often used reindeer of painted lead or plaster covered with leather or fur.

Japan, Germany, and the United States all made items of another type of papier mâché that began to appear in the late 1920s. Called *pressed cardboard,* it resembles old egg-carton material and is the substance of which jack-o'lanterns were made before the advent of plastic. Heavily pressed millboard (similar to fiberboard) or layers of many sheets of paper that had been thoroughly saturated with water were pressed into a mold or shaped over a wooden form or wire frame. Heat-dried and dipped into a solution of linseed oil and tar, they were baked again and then varnished, lacquered, and painted. This method produced figures with a shiny finish. Those with an egg-carton matte surface were not varnished and lacquered but simply painted after being baked.

Santa Claus figures of pressed cardboard were usually copies of the more robust Santa seen in the Coca-Cola ads. They were shaped in various poses: standing, bending, or sitting. All of them had an opening in their backs to hold candy, greens, or gifts. They still turn up occasionally as back stock in old grocery stores where they had once been used as display pieces. Although figures of this material are coarse and not too attractive, to ignore them would be a significant omission from any collection.

The Germans made another kind of Santa figure during this same period, 1920–1930, that, in contrast to those of pressed cardboard, is extremely handsome. This Santa is quite large, measuring up to three feet in height. After World War I, all toys had become simpler in design and detail, and much more attention had been paid to scale. Distinguishing characteristics of these tall Santas are their hand-painted mask faces made of buckram and their "stuffed-mitten" hands. Some of the lifelike facial expressions on these figures equal those of the early 1890 Father Christmas models. They have sensitive human faces. Rarely, one of the figures will have genuine fur eyebrows, in the 1930s called "clown's white," and a beard made of goat's hair. Suit trim was often what manufacturers called "swansdown." One might guess that these Santas were display items as were those made of pressed cardboard. They make impressive holiday decorations anywhere.

Exports from Germany also included large shipments of cardboard (not formed or pressed) candy containers with distinctive ball-shaped bodies, ball-shaped heads capped by paper cones, and half-sphere feet. All surfaces with the exception of the face and the fur beard were covered with paper plush. Their heads wobble on neck springs if moved, and their bodies open to reveal hidden candy. Very common, but very cunning and noteworthy because of their abundance on the market, they began life in the late 1920s and are still made today. Their faces are painted by airbrush. Early containers are marked "Germany"; contemporary ones read "Made in

Western Germany." Needless to say, the earlier pieces have more charm and appeal.

The 1920s also ushered in the era of the milk-glass light bulb from Japan. When Austria was cut off as a source for tree lights during World War I, the Japanese began assembling them in their homes and shipping them to the United States. The Austrian lights were lightweight and transparent before they were painted. Japanese light bulbs were opaque and heavy, poor by comparison. As with so many other products, the Japanese tried to copy the Austrian bulbs, but they failed. Their inferior paint chipped and cracked, and worse yet, when lit, the chips and cracks showed even more! Determined to succeed, and they did, the Japanese tried using blown milk-glass tubing, which involved painting only small areas on a bulb. Fine details were painted on by hand.

Japanese economic conditions gradually improved; a decade later small factories were set up to manufacture the bulbs using small machines purchased from the United States. Thousands of little light bulbs were exported between 1917 and 1941, many of them figural ones. Among the most common and most loved are the Santa Claus bulbs, which were created in many guises—even as St. Nicholas. So cherished are they by some owners today that it matters not one whit whether they work. The owners merely tie a cord around their sockets and hang them on the tree. Collecting Christmas bulbs is one of the newest fields of collecting; it offers plenty of room for newcomers.

Several styles of large Santa Claus bulbs were also produced with standard-size sockets. These are considered choice items, whether or not they still light. Like their smaller Japanese counterparts, they are glass, formed in metal molds. The same techniques were employed in making the large and small lights. Both involved removing the air from the bulb, setting the automatic filament, and airbrushing the paint on the outside. It is thought that they were used either for mantel decorations or as window lights. Window lighting was a common practice during the 1920s and 1930s, as it is in Sweden today.

Between the late 1920s and the beginning of World War II, fine Santa Claus figures in Celluloid were being fabricated in America by several companies that are now impossible to identify. The most prolific was the Irwin Company, located in New York and Chicago. The quality of these American figures is superior: good molding, good styling, and good color. How unfortunate it is to know so little about their manufacturers.

In the 1930s the Americans also produced candy in a fascinating array of glass candy containers, actually small toys that held cheap candy pellets. Even the poorest child in America at one time or another must have parted with a few cents to buy one. The only problem was choosing the candy container you wanted! The earliest candy containers of this type were corked; later ones had metal screw tops. Naturally, Santa Claus was represented, especially at Christmastime, when parents bought them as stocking stuffers for their children. After the war the heads of the Santas were made of plastic, and even later the whole container was. Reproductions of the old glass ones are now being made.

World War II changed the face of Christmas. After peace came, Americans turned to American products. Interior-decorating magazines pushed the new modernity, and households across America followed suit. Christmas trees were laden with turquoise and magenta and pale blue and silver ball ornaments; bows of silver or gold were tucked in between. Strings of lights were tossed out, literally, and moving color wheels, placed in front of a tree, cast changes of color onto the tree as they revolved. Elegant holiday tables were set with centerpieces of silver or gold artificial fruit or colored ball ornaments, tied up with the ubiquitous bows. The centerpiece usually rested on a rectangle of blue mirrored glass and was often accompanied by a fleet of mercury-glass reindeer. For the first time American machines at Corning Glass in New York were churning out Christmas ball ornaments by the millions.

The garbage men of America removed box after box of old Christmas "stuff" that people threw out to make room for the new mass-produced ornaments. These boxes contained old Father Christmas figures, fragile and lovely antique ornaments from Germany, Austria, Czechoslovakia, and Poland, charming Japanese Christmas lights along with thousands of Japanese Santas—much of what had been so beautiful and handcrafted in Christmases past. They were lost forever. Even an appreciation of what was gone took decades to sink in to the American consciousness. What remained of old Christmas decor had been kept only through sentiment or indifference, pushed aside in the attic.

A few Santa figures trickled in from the U.S. Occupied Zone of Germany during the four years of its life. Europe was recovering from a devastating period, trying to rebuild and find some order in the shambles. Remnants of Old World craftsmanship remained, but the plastic, battery-operated age had arrived, and there was no reprieve.

The Japanese recovered more quickly and stepped forward with innovative ideas, no longer content to

5. On a scale of one to ten, this figure would have to be a ten in anyone's collection. He is representative of an extremely small group of "white-wadding" Father Christmas figures with paper-covered wire hands. Another such figure is known: that Father Christmas carries an ancient grapevine wreath in place of the basket that is shown here. German, cotton-wadding Father Christmas, composition face and berries, paper over wire hands, fabric feet, fiber basket, crepe-paper bag, H. 13½", c. 1890.

be imitators in the toy field. Their factories and designers produced windup and battery-operated Santas, brightly colored and able to move in ingenious ways. Japan rapidly acquired world dominance of the tin toy industry. It is interesting to compare two postwar toys, both Santas-in-a-box, made at the same time. The German Santa jumps out of his box on a spring when a button is pushed; the Japanese version is key-wound and Santa rises and falls smoothly out of his box, bobbing his head as he keeps appearing and disappearing in the chimney.

The Japanese also reissued their standing Santa Claus figures that had been so loved in the 1920s and 1930s. The new ones were stiff-spined in a curious way, with a tendency to lean forward. Gone were the roughly modeled clay faces, now replaced by either plastic or painted cardboard faces. The cardboard was not molded, but applied, shieldlike, to the head, and the skin tones were off-color. The facial paint had a definite orangish tint. A collector would never look twice at them were it not for their historical interest.

Mechanical battery-operated Santas "Made in the U.S.A." were found in toy shops and novelty stores during the 1950s and 1960s. Although they could not perform the antics of Japanese models, they were nonetheless interesting and amusing. Many merely raise an arm to ring a Christmas handbell or drink a glass of Coca-Cola. Unlike the typically small Japanese mechanicals, most American ones were approximately one-and-a-half feet tall.

Madison Avenue, during this same time, controlled the buying habits of the American public; it used 3-D Santas with plastic faces and distinctive rayon-velvet suits to promote many products. These Santas contrasted with the large stand-up cardboard Santas of an earlier era. The Madison Avenue Santas had unusually curly, carded-wool beards. Some even appeared to be marcelled!

Using Santa as an advertising gimmick was not original to the 1950s. A hundred and twenty-five years earlier, children had read of holiday toys in popular magazine ads at yuletide. By 1900 Santa was a regular pitchman in household weeklies, appearing with everything from Waterman's pens and Bradley's dart games to New Home sewing machines to Cream of Wheat. One advertisement read, "Good old St. Nick knows that Cream of Wheat is best for boys and girls." In later decades Santa promoted Coca-Cola in a big way.

In the 1960s Christmas took a back seat to the political upheaval that racked the nation. It was peace marches, not Santa Claus, Kent State, not

Christmas, that held the public's attention. This period also saw a relative scarcity of fine Christmas items. Taiwan, a latecomer in the field, increased its quotas of cheap, poorly made holiday goods. West German ornaments, for the most part, were carelessly molded and painted. The best came from East Germany and Italy, but supplies were limited.

After the passing of the Vietnam period, America in the 1970s tried to forget the changes it had faced a decade earlier. It looked for security and sought it in the memory of a safer, gentler time. America reached back into its heritage and began to collect all parts of it, to hug it close. It remembered the warmth of childhood Christmas celebrations and rediscovered the beauty of old Christmas things. The hunt was on for collectibles; it seemed as if everyone in America was involved in collecting something. Christmas figures began to be highly regarded as great finds. The earliest ones were now cherished as desirable folk art. Indeed, all Christmas items became collectible: old crèches, putzes, early Christmas lights, strings of figural light bulbs, old ornaments of every kind.

Interest in them grew near the end of the decade, not only because of their innate appeal, but because of a general decline in religious practices. Santa and gift giving had replaced the Nativity scene for many people, especially the young.

In the 1980s collecting is now undertaken with more care and a greater sense of leisure. Inflation has reduced the disposable income buyers can spend, and prices are high for what fine collectibles can be found. This is particularly true of Christmas figures, for the supply of the old lovely ones is very small indeed.

What are the alternatives? One can purchase contemporary figures or search out the fine reproductions being made by today's artisans. The patina of age is missing from them, of course, but, festooned with holiday greens, they can be pleasing substitutes. Furthermore, they may become the treasures of the future.

New collectors may wish to seek out only contemporary figures from around the world that represent Santa or Old Man Christmas. The Scandinavians provide the most whimsical ones. *Jultomten* from Sweden, *Julesvenn* from Norway, and *Julnisse* from Denmark are the gift giving elves, red-clad figures with pointed caps and long white whiskers. These elves are seen in store windows filled with hay, a reminder of hay-filled barns where they live for the remainder of the year. They are mischievous creatures and perform bad tricks in a household unless appeased by

good deeds. When all is well, they will protect the animals and guard the house from harm throughout the year.

*Jultomten* rides a goat named *Julbock*, *Julnisse* rides *Jul-buken*. These goats have pagan roots, being modeled after the goat of Thor that pulled its master's chariot. Straw goat figures are seen everywhere in Sweden and Denmark at Christmastime. A remarkable two-story-high wooden goat stood at the entrance to one of Stockholm's major shopping centers in 1981.

Scandinavian Santa figures show the fine design typical of these countries. Some are sleek wood carvings, others are stuffed toy figures with vinyl or Sculpey (a commercial modeling compound) faces and hands, and others are made of wood and hemp. There is a great variety available; all are expensive. It is interesting that few crèche scenes are to be found in Scandinavia.

Russian figures are among the most fascinating pieces produced today. *Ded Moroz*, Grandfather Frost, is the Russian Spirit of winter and Russia's modern gift giver who brings presents to Russian children on New Year's Day. Because Russia has been under a largely atheistic regime since the Revolution of 1917, Christmas is chiefly a nonreligious celebration. Father Christmas was the name of the old Russian Santa Claus, and the new figure of Grandfather Frost bears more than a little resemblance to him. He is old and wears long robes and a flat-crowned hat typical of the ancient *Rus*. Very occasionally, a figure will wear a red robe; it is more customary to see Grandfather Frost attired in pale, wintry colors. These Russian figures are not usually seen outside Russia, where they are only available at holidaytide.

In Hungary, a Russian satellite nation, the celebration of Christmas has also been largely suppressed. A few stalls selling meager Christmas decorations—twisted candles, skeins of tinsel, a plastic Santa Claus—were seen on the busy streets of Budapest in 1982. Infrequently, a Hungarian figure is made for export, whereas the East Germans produce many Santa figures to be sent to the West.

The majority of new Santa figures from East Germany are either glass ornaments or are figures made of wood from the Erzgebirge region. The wooden ones resemble older versions. The most exciting East German Father Christmas in recent years has to be a hand puppet from Dresden, made of felt and hand-painted.

Italy has been unique in that over the decades three different personages have evolved as the gift givers of Christmas. On Christmas Eve, gifts within the close family circle have traditionally been brought by the *Gesù Bambino.* But the duty of distributing gifts on a large scale falls upon *La Befana,* the much revered old witch of olden times, who, like her European counterparts, miraculously comes down the chimney on Epiphany Eve (January 5) with her sack of of goodies and her broom! Very few antique *La Befana* figures turn up today, but the new ones of vinyl and cheap cloth (always holding a broom!) abound at Christmastime. They are seen in many stalls of the Rome Christmas market at the Piazza Navona. A third fellow, the *Babbo Natale,* is more like the old German Father Christmas, although it is not molded like the early German ones. Italian craftsmen produce this figure today, made of painted papier mâché, and it is available in the United States in several styles. The exact method of manufacture is uncertain, but it appears as if the cap and robes are formed of paper that has, in some way, been dipped into a hardening solution, allowed to dry, and painted. In any case, the finished figure is handsome and exhibits subtle coloring.

Mexico and Spain, in sharp contrast to Scandinavia, emphasize the *Nacimiento* rather than the secular aspects of the Christmas season. Santa Claus hardly pauses over these countries except in the homes of the craftsmen making Santa figures for export. In Spain the few Santas for sale at the Christmas markets are made of pieces of logs sliced vertically with wooden sticks crudely attached as legs. Their faces are pieces of red and black felt glued onto the cut end of the log. A red-and-black felt hat hangs precariously over one eye. These are hardly big sellers! Mexican Santas, on the other hand, are so colorful and eye-catching that their commercial success is assured. They are created from tin, cut and finished so that no sharp edges remain. Mexican tinsmiths have presented their Santas in fresh, novel situations that are happy and entertaining. One Santa rides in an automobile, leaning back like an entrepreneur. Another appears timidly riding a tin bicycle. They are lacquered in typical bright Mexican colors: orange, purple, red, turquoise, and shocking pink. Similar Santa tree ornaments of flat tin are also made, but these have none of the gaiety of the three-dimensional figures. Santa *piñatas* of bright tissue paper over a papier-mâché base are another popular Mexican Christmas product, easy to find and sure to please! These are available in many poses.

Figures from Central America are quite similar to the clay Nativity figures and Tree of Life candelabra made in Mexico. It would be impossible to guess the country of origin of a small Santa figure made in El Salvador, were it not for the marking on the base. The sunny colors are typically Mexican. The Santa

carries a tree decorated with small clay balls as ornaments that are attached to the tree by thin wires, which is the same technique used by Mexican potters in making haloes around the heads of religious figures and attaching flowers and leaves to clay pieces.

Further south, Ecuadoran artisans have perfected the art of making figures from bread and sugar. Their Santa figures exhibit great panache. Formed and baked, then painted and varnished with a high-gloss finish, they are a modern art form. The finishing detail, made of the dough and attached to the matrix of the piece, is marvelous. Ecuadorans also weave Santas of straw both as tree ornaments and as freestanding figures. Their ability to mold body contours in closely woven patterns is remarkable. Like the Mexican and El Salvadoran Santas, the Ecuadoran Santas are exported all over the world.

In contrast to the figures currently being made in the Western Hemisphere, Austrian and West German figures at the present time are traditionally styled. The models, however, wear garments of synthetic fabric—orlon pile—and have plastic bodies. They carry trees made of artificial materials. While the quality of the *Weihnachtsmann* is only fair, the total effect, with a bag full of candy on his back, is engaging. The Germans also have continued to make Steiff Santa figures, not too unlike earlier ones. All possess the famous round metal tab in the ear, which is the company trademark.

In the United States during the 1960s comic-strip and cartoon characters captured the attention of Americans of all ages. Two favorites were Superman, and Snoopy from the immensely popular *Peanuts* cartoon strip. Both SuperSantas and Snoopy Santas made their appearance and sold well to their fans. In the same class were the Hallmark tin Santas, part of a larger, annual ornament offering made by this famous greeting card company. This Santa, and another from the Chein Industries, were big sellers in the early 1980s. The Bristol Ware Division of Chein Industries manufactured and sold a roly-poly Santa that was a reproduction of an old tobacco tin. The beautiful chromolithography on the piece made it a winner, and it has continued to be a successful product.

Other American business firms have produced dressed Santa figures. One with great sales appeal was made by My Favorite Things of Carmel, California. Its popularity has resulted from superior stitchery and the use of first-rate materials. The Santa emanates warmth. Another was made and introduced by Faith Wick of Grand Rapids, Michigan. This Santa has a sensitive bisque face and a rich, red robe. The largest and oldest of all companies making Santa figures is Annalee in New Hampshire. Family-owned, it was incorporated in 1954. The Santas Annalee manufactures are constructed of felt with a flexible wire armature for positioning. Originally hand-painted, the Santa faces are now painted by machine. Their Santas have been used at the White House and have even decorated a Neiman-Marcus Christmas gift to Queen Elizabeth II. Although angel forms have long been their trademark, Santa Claus figures have been identified with Annalee since the beginning of the company.

A quick look through current Christmas catalogues reveals that Taiwan is making far more Christmas figures than any other country. The quality of the figures varies depending on the price tag and which American firm commissions the work. In general, the bisque Santa figurines are quite good. The molding is detailed, the bisque smooth, the finishing neat. But something is lacking. Perhaps in the attempt to make them appear old, their makers chose to paint them in washed-out colors, making them look wan. The red-coated Santas come off better than the others. These Taiwanese figures, despite their lack of punch, can be used to good effect with greens and other accessories in holiday decorating.

Handcrafted Father Christmas and Santa figures are quite different from the machine-made products offered today. Made by craftsmen all over America, no two are alike. From the Midwest comes a delightful soft sculpture dressed in old wool robes. Yellowed white wool was purchased at a local Goodwill store and fashioned into his costume. Another from the Midwest is elegant. He has a strong face, and touches of mink fur on his blue velvet robes make him almost regal. A very attractive touch is a bag filled with miniature toys and candy. Standing an imposing fourteen inches high, he is a magnificent mantel decoration for the Advent season.

Simpler in feeling but just as elegant is a wood-carved Father Christmas, patterned after the old Lauschan models. Rays of light catch in the shadows

6. Any papier-mâché figure from this period is a treasure. This is the German prototype; he was made in various sizes. German, painted papier-mâché Father Christmas, finished with mica sprinkles, H. 4″, 1890s.

of his face and robe, calling to mind the old austere gift giver of the nineteenth century. Some people might prefer a plaster version of Old Man Christmas, beautiful under a glass dome.

If a person chooses to collect these Christmas figures or decides to own just one or two to add holiday cheer to his or her life, where can they be found? New figures, of course, pose no problem, and the choices are infinite. Advertisements in interior-decorating magazines, holiday catalogues, gift shops, flower shops, stationery and greeting card stores, five-and-dimes, and discount houses—all feature the less-expensive Christmas men. Some handmade figures may also be available from these sources and from holiday bazaars. However, because artisans often make only one-of-a-kind Santas, news of their whereabouts travels only by word of mouth. Imported figures can usually be located in exclusive boutiques. Better still, friends about to set out on a journey can probably be deputized to purchase them abroad.

The motto of the U.S. Army Service Forces is "The difficult we do immediately. The impossible takes a little longer." How true this is, but it *is* possible to find the antique Christmas figures! As is true for many old things, the best source remains the house sale where the owners have cleaned out an attic untouched for years. Prices are often lowest there. Rummage sales and flea markets are also often surprisingly fertile fields. Helpful friends and other collectors should not be underestimated as avenues to new finds. Those determined to find a beautiful old figure will not flinch at antiques shop price tags. Sage advice to all collectors is never to expect too much. The search often leads to nothing, but occasionally the pot of gold will be at the end of the rainbow.

If a person is collecting Santa figures in earnest and is new to the game, how can he or she be sure of buying a genuinely old Father Christmas or Santa Claus? First it must be examined carefully, noting the regularity of the features. Handcrafted items are as individual as their makers. The material used in making the figure will probably show real signs of age, not an overlay of antiquing solution. The figures probably will not be too bright, although some figures have never been taken from their original boxes and can be "good as new." Sometimes the figure actually smells of mothballs, or of cedar from a chest, or is just plain musty from having been in storage too long! To the collector that whiff of age is a heady fragrance!

Rarely, a Christmas figure will be marked with a label giving a country of origin. Germans were more disposed to mark their products, using either "Germany," "Made in the U.S. Zone of Occupied Germany," "West Germany," or "German Democratic Republic." Remember, labels fall off and markings become distorted. On occasion, marking and labels get covered over by the felt that is often glued on a base to prevent scratching a table surface. A word to those who may be inspired to create Santa figures themselves. It is the responsibility of the artisans to sign and date their work, for two reasons: novices deserve to know what they are buying, and future generations will enjoy knowing when and by whom a piece was made. This plea cannot be stressed enough!

Because styles of figures can be misleading, too, other details need to be considered in the effort to determine all that it is possible to know about a figure. The material used in making the face is a helpful clue. Is it papier-mâché, composition, clay, plastic, vinyl, felt, cotton, Sculpey, bisque, or wood? And if there should be a tiny hole in a stuffed figure, see what type of filling was used. There is a significant difference among straw, kapok, old cotton, felt cotton, fiberfill, and shredded foam. All had their periods of usefulness.

If chromolithographed "scrap" faces and hands are used on a figure, check to see if the scrap is made of thick paper. That is one indication of age. Turn it over, if possible, to see if it has yellowed with age. Old scrap usually has.

Old or new, handcrafted or machine-made, genuine or fabricated, Eastern or Western, any Santa can win the heart of the right owner. As in love, beauty is in the eye of the beholder. The old bewhiskered gentleman is the inevitable symbol of Christmas, no matter in what guise he appears. Is there anyone who can question the answer that the editor of *The New York Sun* wrote to Virginia O'Hanlon in 1897, when she wrote to ask him if, indeed, there was a Santa Claus? This reply by Francis P. Church to the doubtful young girl sums up all that is best about Santa Claus:

Yes, Virginia, there is a Santa Claus. He exists as certainly as love and generosity and devotion exist, and you know that they abound and give to your life its highest beauty and joy. Alas! how dreary would be the world if there were no Santa Claus! It would be as dreary as if there were no Virginias. No Santa Claus! Thank God, he lives, and lives forever. A thousand years from now, Virginia, nay, 10 times 10,000 years from now, he will continue to make glad the heart of childhood.

7. Perhaps the red wool cap was added to this classic Father Christmas by a later generation, but the hood fits precisely and therefore may be original. He is standing among very old Christmas lights, which hung on tree branches before the advent of clip-on candles. German, papier-mâché Father Christmas, covered with mica, red wool hood, *Erikamoos* (dried and dyed bog heather) tree, gold tinsel on base, H. 9½", 1890–1900.

8. "Santa Claus is not a myth; he is very much alive and has a capacity of 60,000,000 man-power in the U.S. alone." So wrote *Good Housekeeping* in a Christmas issue in 1888. This magnificent fellow is on his rounds, visiting homes of all children—both rich and poor. A Father Christmas of this caliber and size is rare, and the touches of gold and mica add elegance to his already imposing stature. German, papier-mâché Father Christmas candy container, painted features, rabbit-fur beard, twig switches, H. 22", c. 1890.

19

9. Dickens described Old Man Christmas in *A Christmas Carol* (1843) as wearing a holly wreath. Shortly after, a German engraver, Moritz von Schwind, drew a hooded figure of Winter walking along the snowy streets as the Christmas man. On his hood rested a wreath of leaves. By the second half of the nineteenth century, many illustrations in magazines showed him bewreathed in holly and ivy. This tradition, short-lived as it was, probably harks back to pagan days and the use of the old circular sun symbol of the holly wreath. Figures with a wreath on the hood are scarce and choice. German, plaster over papier-mâché, rabbit-fur beard, chenille trim, goose-feather tree, H. 12″, c. 1890.

10, 11, 12. Red and white are the traditional colors Germans preferred to use on their papier-mâché Father Christmas figures. On rare occasions they dipped their brushes into pots of green or lavender, gold, pale pink, or blue. Competition is keen in the search to unearth these lovely colored figures. All German, plaster over papier-mâché Father Christmas figures. Top: candy container, mica-covered, goose-feather tree, composition berry, 7″ tall, 1890–1910. Center: fur beard, flannel suit and cap, string belt, straw basket, base marked "Made in Germany," 4″ tall, c. 1910. Bottom: mica trim on figure, goose-feather tree, composition berries, H. 12″, 1890s.

13, 14. A limited series of early Father Christmas figures possess smooth, florid complexions that set them apart from the usual papier-mâché Christmas figures. They are composed of a papier-mâché base with an overlay of plaster. Quite often these figures carry a basket, which the Germans term *die Kiepe*. German, plaster over papier-mâché Father Christmas figures. Top: fur beard, canton-flannel suit with fur trim, gold twine belt, wooden sticks, 12″ tall, c. 1890. Bottom: fur beard, canton-flannel suit and cap with flannel trim, replaced tree, H. 9″, c. 1890.

15. He came down that chimney? Of course he did! Another figure made of plaster over papier-mâché, our old friend landed in a Nürnberg kitchen. These kitchens were beloved toys of German children, first made in 1840. The one pictured here with Father Christmas was made after 1850, as the designs on the walls are embossed, not stenciled like the earliest models. German, painted plaster over papier-mâché Father Christmas, face, hands, and boots, velvet suit with flannel trim, fur beard, goose-feather tree, wooden base, H. 7″, c. 1900.

16. Another "basket" Father Christmas, this one is distinguished by the dapper stitched-on pockets of his coat. German, plaster over papier-mâché Father Christmas, face, hands, and boots, flannel suit with string belt, goose-feather tree, basket on back (die Kiepe), H. 12″, c. 1890.

17. Mastery in papier-mâché—the molding in this piece is so fantastic that this Father Christmas seems almost human. Unfortunately, he is only a torso, although banked in a wreath of greens he would make a spectacular Christmas display. German, painted plaster over papier-mâché Father Christmas upper body, chenille trim, H. 14½", 1890–1900.

18. Signs of the season: Santa Claus and a set of children's nesting blocks. Father Christmas is comely in his floor-length robe, ornamented by the electrified lantern hanging from his string belt. German, Father Christmas candy container, papier-mâché face, hands, and feet, rabbit-fur beard, string belt, electrified lantern, goose-feather tree, wooden base, H. 14", c. 1900.

24

19. Victorian animal pull-toys were quite common around the end of the nineteenth century. Illustrations of toys under the Christmas tree rarely fail to show one. It is extremely uncommon, however, to find a Father Christmas and a sleigh on a base with wheels. The sponge sleigh is also unique. German, papier-mâché Father Christmas, trimmed with mica flakes, H. 9″; papier-mâché reindeer with pewter antlers. Wooden baseboard (L. 21″) with iron wheels, c. 1890.

20. A prominent widow's hump makes this Pelze-Nicol truly wonderful! The gross exaggeration of his hump augments his already austere face as he holds on to his switches and carefully calculates his coal provisions. Will there be enough? German, very humped Pelze-Nicol or Belsnickle, papier-mâché face, hands, and boots, rabbit-fur beard, canton-flannel suit, lamb's-wool trim, string belt, twigs, H. 10″, 1890.

21. "Pelze-Nicol" translated literally means "Nicholas dressed in fur." Actually, all Christmas figures that are dressed in fur or that are grotesquely misshapen fall into this category. All North German children regarded Pelze-Nicol as a terror, the punishing figure who knew all their sins through the Christ Child. When German immigrants settled the Pennsylvania German communities in the New World, the pronunciation of Pelze-Nicol gradually eroded into Belsnickle, which has remained to this day. German, plaster over papier-mâché Pelze-Nicol, or Belsnickle, rabbit-fur beard, genuine fur coat, goose-feather tree, wooden base, H. 10″, 1895–1900.

22. This funny little Santa has a mysterious face of "scrap" and no visible means of locomotion! German, Father Christmas, scrap face, crepe-paper suit and hood, fur beard; mica-covered painted cardboard sleigh, cord reins, 3″ x 7½″, c. 1900.

26

23, 24. Both Nicholas men here wear showy coats in the tradition of old Pelze-Nicol, although they are not the usual twisted, fierce figures associated with him. Actually, the plaid coat and leather pouch on Old Man Christmas (top) turn him into a fashion plate. The white coat of plush makes Father Christmas (bottom) quite elegant, too, as he goes about his duties of checking on cookie supplies. He and the Oreos he surveys were made at about the same time. German, Father Christmas figures, plaster over papier-mâché faces, hands, and boots, rabbit-fur beards, both carrying goose-feather trees. Top: wearing mohair coat and leather pouch, H. 8½", 1890s. Bottom: wearing plush coat, H. 6½", 1895–1900.

25. Made to hang from a tree branch, this Father Christmas, bundled up in his voluminous cotton-wadding robe with Dresden buttons, reminds us of college men in their fabulous old raccoon coats. The figure here has an armature of cardboard to support his opulent garment. German, Father Christmas, scrap face, tinted cotton-wadding robe (mica-covered), Dresden buttons, cardboard feet, H. 7″, c. 1890.

26. Lauscha, in the Thuringian mountains of Germany, was the center of the cottage industry making both glass and cotton-wadding tree ornaments. Cotton ornaments were the traditional favorites of children; made in many different fanciful designs, the most popular were the Nicholas men. German, Nicholas men. Left: scrap face, cotton-wadding body, crepe-paper hat, H. 5½″, 1890–1910. Right: scrap face, cotton-wadding body, *Erikamoos* tree, H. 5″, 1890–1910.

27, 28. Both of these Christmas men were most likely used as store decorations or in window displays. The pressed-cardboard figure (top) has been reproduced, but modern copies cannot capture the gentle coloring and patina of the old embossed piece. Father Christmas (bottom) is an example of die-cut chromolithography with a scrap face. He is taller than most scrap items. Both German. Top: painted pressed cardboard, cardboard fold-out stand on back, H. 9¾", c. 1910. Bottom: die-cut chromolithographic Father Christmas with scrap face, torso, and boots, pleated tissue-paper skirt, crepe-paper trim, foil stars, H. 19⅜", 1890–1910.

29. Over the years roly-poly toys have been made in many media—Celluloid, formed cardboard, tin, and plastic. The early papier-mâché Santa here was hand-made and hand-painted. He plays a little three-tone tune as he rolls around on his base. German, papier-mâché Santa, painted, H. 8½″, c. 1900.

30. "Christmas would not be Christmas without candy for little children and also those of a larger growth," counseled a *Good Housekeeping* article in December 1891. Chocolate Santas, favorite sweets of Victorians, were made by hand from metal molds and were available in diverse designs and sizes. Reproductions of the old molds are being made today, but they are lighter and offer much less detail. Left to right, tin molds with metal side clips: 1. German, stooped Father Christmas, H. 7¾″, 1890–1910. 2. German, St. Nicholas, H. 5″, 1890–1910. 3. American, Santa Claus, H. 12″, 1980 reproduction. 4. German, Father Christmas, H. 6″, c. 1890. 5. German, weary Father Christmas, H. 6″, c. 1890.

31. Beginning in the eighteenth century, German housewives molded *Weihnachtsmänner* of *Eierzucken,* a combination of egg white, starch, rose water, and tragacanth. It was an excellent medium, as it dried hard and white, kept a long time, and could be painted. By the beginning of the nineteenth century, figures such as the one pictured here were in wide use in Germany as tree and table decorations. German, egg sugar Father Christmas, molded and mounted on a cookie base *(Oblaten),* H. 9½", 1919.

32. Each country celebrating Christmas pridefully attests to the superiority of its holiday cake, plum pudding, and cookie recipes. The favorite homemade cookie in America is a moot point. Old-fashioned butter cookies rank high, cut out with some of the old tin Santa cutters seen here. German, tin Santa Claus cookie cutters. Left: H. 3½". Center: H. 9". Right: H. 4½", early twentieth century.

33. It is difficult to know whether this Santa is a handmade or commercial product. He does have, however, the look of figures made between 1910 and 1920. Not a roly-poly, he is merely a gourd whose contents have dried out, leaving him extremely lightweight. Unknown origin, painted-gourd Santa, H. 4¼", 1910–1920.

34. Banks are the second most collectible items sought after today; mechanical ones are more fascinating and therefore are more expensive. The Father Christmas bank shown here is choice. Made by J. and E. Stevens and patented October 15, 1889, it is cast iron. As a lever is pulled, the hand is depressed and puts the coin in the chimney. Santa's pack is filled with horns, whistles, and other toys, embossed into the casting of his pack. Modern reproductions are being made. American, hand-painted, cast-iron Santa-at-chimney mechanical bank, reads "Santa Claus" on base of chimney, screw opening underneath, toys embossed on bag; Santa H. 6", chimney 3½" x 1½", 1888.

35. Blown-glass Father Christmas and Santa Claus ornaments were first made during the 1880s in a little German village named Lauscha. Its townspeople engaged in many cottage crafts, but the major one was the glass-ornament industry. A new gasworks, built in Lauscha in 1867, allowed the glassblowers to form thin-walled, light glass objects for the first time as they at last had a steadily regulated flame. (Their old lamps, which burned turnip oil, were unreliable.) Soon glassblowers were creating many beautiful ornaments in a wide array of designs. Once Americans discovered the new ornaments, they demanded more and more of them. They had become the rage in America by 1910. The ornaments were sold by the "publisher" system, the publisher being the middleman between the manufacturer and the retailer. A publisher today would be called a wholesaler. He sold house-to-house or by mail order. An alternate system was the "buyer" system, in which an American buyer went to Lauscha and bought directly from publisher to publisher. One American chose another method. F. W. Woolworth, the American dime-store tycoon, went to Lauscha and bought from the glassblowers in their own homes. He sent home millions of glass ornaments over the years to retail in his own stores throughout America. Skilled German blowers cornered the market until the 1920s, when Austria and Czechoslovakia entered the field competitively. They were joined later by Poland. But it is the German ornaments, such as the ones seen here, that are sought after by Christmas aficionados. They were created during the Golden Age of glass Christmas ornaments—1880 to 1920. They are lovely, fragile—and breakable! Consequently, their numbers have diminished over the years, and they are both scarce and costly. Fortunately, Father Christmas and Santa figures were often made in glass, and they are more readily found than other figures. German, glass tree ornaments with metal hangers, H. 3″–6″, goose-feather tree, 1890s–1920s.

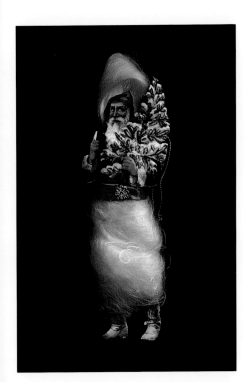

36. It is hard to believe that the spun glass used in making this figure was spun by hand. It required both skill and long hours. These figures are extremely fragile as there is nothing but dabs of glue, now nearly a hundred years old, holding the various sections together. Care must be taken not to snag the spun glass, because once a strand has been dislodged it is almost impossible to smooth it back into place. It is remarkable that the admonishing finger on his right hand, made of paper, has managed to survive. German, spun-glass Father Christmas, scrap face, torso, legs, feet, tree, and belt, gold-paper buckle, H. 6½″, c. 1895.

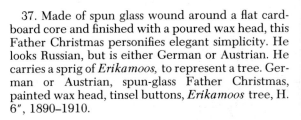

37. Made of spun glass wound around a flat cardboard core and finished with a poured wax head, this Father Christmas personifies elegant simplicity. He looks Russian, but is either German or Austrian. He carries a sprig of *Erikamoos*, to represent a tree. German or Austrian, spun-glass Father Christmas, painted wax head, tinsel buttons, *Erikamoos* tree, H. 6″, 1890–1910.

38. This is an exceptional Father Christmas, a "nodder." His underpinnings are constructed of very heavy wire and blocks of wood. When squeezed in the midsection, his head is moved forward and backward by a primitive spring mechanism. His beard, molded as a unit with his head, juts forward in a strange way. A similar Father Christmas whose head and body move freely without manipulation is known to exist; this type of figure is a "double nodder." Nodders of any kind are very scarce. German, Father Christmas nodder, heavy composition head, iron hands, new flannel gown with gilt trim and Dresden buttons (copied from original), H. 7″, 1902.

39. Exhibiting the same peculiar beard conformation as that shown on the nodder in plate 38, this charming old St. Nicholas is dressed in all the regalia of the old bishop. His embroidered cape sets off his crepe-paper undergarments nicely. German, St. Nicholas, plaster head, hands, and crozier cap, cloth miter and cape, crepe-paper undergarments, paper trim, wooden crozier staff, H. 7″, c. 1900–1910.

40. Wonderful old *Sint Niklass*, shown here without his traditional robe and miter, is the beloved gift giver to all Dutch children. They place two wooden shoes on the hearth on December 5, St. Nicholas's Eve. One shoe is filled with wishes for things they hope the saint will bring, the other with straw, bread, or beans for St. Nicholas's white horse. When the horse eats the hay, it is replaced with goodies and gifts for the children. Dutch, St. Nicholas, painted cloth face, fur beard, cloth body, leather belt, wooden shoes, H. 12½″, c. 1910.

41, 42. Many Christmas figures of this period wore felt clothing, unlike earlier ones commonly dressed in canton flannel. Father Christmas (top) standing in his long coat amid a set of very old and stern marionettes, is considered a fairly scarce figure. His face is a good example of how the Germans used red lines around the eyes and on the forehead to intensify facial expression. A candy container is hidden beneath his coat. The spry fellow at the bottom is flexible, being made on a heavy wire armature, which facilitates his rest stops on the long journey south. Both German, papier-mâché faces, hands, and feet, rabbit-fur beards. Top: Father Christmas candy container, felt cap and coat, remnant of goose-feather tree, wooden base, H. 12″, 1910–1920. Bottom: Santa on wire armature, felt cap and suit, string belt, goose-feather tree, H. 5¼″, 1910–1930.

43, 44. Cinema director Ingmar Bergman's memorable 1983 film, *Fanny and Alexander,* is supposedly autobiographical, and among other things it portrays a glorious 1907 family Christmas celebration during his childhood in Sweden. Viewed twice during the film is a great Father Christmas that combines the characteristics of the two wonderful ones pictured here. The Bergman figures resemble those in plate 44, but they are mechanical and bob up and down like those in plate 43. The figures in plate 43 were photographed in Stockholm and may be either German or Swedish. Top: probably German, perhaps Swedish, Father Christmas with wooden face, painted eyes, flannel suit with fur trim, fur mittens, composition boots; reindeer with glass eyes, reindeer-fur-covered body, natural stag horns and hoofs, missing reins, 18″ x 24″, c. 1900. Reindeer is a key-wind nodder. Bottom: German, Father Christmas, papier-mâché face, hands, and boots, fur beard, canton-flannel cap and suit, missing tree; slightly flocked and painted plaster reindeer, lead antlers. Bottom: overall H.: 15″, c. 1900.

45. Old Man Christmas would never miss a visit to any children, especially those out on the prairie. He is there now! Composed of plaster over papier-mâché, this plate shows especially well how the density of the medium gives brilliance and depth to the painted finish of the figure. German, plaster over papier-mâché Father Christmas, goose-feather tree, H. 6½", 1900–1910.

46. Great character could be achieved in molded Celluloid, as this superb example of German workmanship attests. Dilute Celluloid was used to paint the features on the face. German, Celluloid face, cotton-wadding suit with flannel trim, goose-feather tree, H. 8½", c. 1900–1910.

47. Father Christmas here is standing by an antique fence and gate, often used by the Germans in putz scenes. The putz is an adaptation of the Nativity scene that grew over the years into an elaborate village scene at Christmastime. It included people, animals, houses, and vegetation, and usually was encircled by a metal fence like the one here. German, Father Christmas candy container. Plaster over papier-mâché face, hands, and boots, rabbit-fur beard, felt suit, leather belt, H. 9″, c. 1910.

48, 49. Many people collect only "snowball" items—either snowballs with figures on them or figures involved in some way with snowballs. Both Santas here are snowball candy containers. The figure on the left is trimmed with glass beads called "Venetian Dew" by the Germans. The Santa on the right is in pristine condition, which increases its value. German candy containers. Left: painted composition figure and snowball, trimmed with glass beads, H. 3½″, 1910–1920. Right: scrap face, cotton-wadding body and snowballs, fabric holly and composition berries, crepe-paper hat, satin ribbon, cardboard-box base (opens), H. 7″, c. 1910.

50. Who wouldn't be agitated if he had to stand in this position forever? Surely old Father Christmas is reaching to remove toys from his pack, not to scratch a perpetual itch! His strange position makes this Santa stand out from a crowd, as does his coat, which is flocked. German, painted papier-mâché Father Christmas, flocked coat and hat with chenille trim, H. 10″, c. 1910.

51. Some papier-mâché Father Christmas figures of this period are wider and more portly than the classic ones; this is one example. German, all papier-mâché Father Christmas, string belt, goose-feather tree, H. 11″, 1900–1910.

52. Cherished toys, worn and well loved, of a long-ago child include a favorite Santa-in-a-box. He pops up when the front knob is depressed and retracts when he is shoved down; the lid relocks. German, Santa jump-up in box, composition face, felt hat and trim, cloth bag, cardboard box covered with *faux* brick paper, H. 7½″, 1910–1920.

53, 54. All Germans share a deep love for their forests; they often made candy boxes featuring Santas on wood in some form. Here are two, one on a log and another on a pile of lumber. Both impart the wintry chill of Christmastime and both open to reveal tasty treats. Both German candy containers. Top: Paper-mâché face, rabbit-fur beard, flannel suit and cap, wooden log, simulated paper age rings, H. 5″, 1920s. Bottom: As above, except for wooden logs of cut tree branches, H. 4″, 1910–1920.

55. He comes on the stroke of midnight! Although the Danes have a Christmas spirit called *Julnisse,* they also enjoyed Old Father Christmas. A beautiful one appears here, exhibiting cool and elegant workmanship in painted plaster. Danish, Santa-in-a-sleigh (H. 4¾") and reindeer (H. 4½") of plaster on wire construction (one antler missing), string reins, leather whip and stoneboat, wooden bases, c. 1910–1920.

56. A great rarity, the Père Noël here looks almost like an old gargoyle with his ghoulish eyes, oversize hood, and very small feet. His beard, which juts forward, is typical of this period. If he were German, which he is not, he would certainly be considered a Belsnickle figure. French, Père Noël papier-mâché face (painted in watercolors) and boots, hood, suit, and gloves of cotton wadding, real switches, H. 14", c. 1910.

57. To compare these two Father Christmas heads is basically to compare the workmanship of Germany and Japan. The fantastic one on the right, when lit, conveys all the mystique of Christmas and casts an eerie light on all whose yearly good deeds hang in the balance. The cruder Japanese head is merely grotesque; the jaws move up and down on a wire spring—in somewhat the same way trick dentures from a magic store clatter when wound up. Right: German, painted plaster Father Christmas tree light, sheet-gelatin eyes and teeth, wire hanger, opening holds tree candle, 3″ x 6″, 1890–1910. Left: Japanese, Santa Claus ashtray, painted bisque, weighted wire device for opening jaw, H. 4″, 1930s.

58. Before the Revolution in 1917 Russian Christmases had a warm yuletide flavor with each village sharing snow games, sleighing parties, carols, and the arrival of Father Christmas. After 1917 Old Man Christmas was gradually replaced by Grandfather Frost. Russian, Father Christmas in two versions, painted carved wood, H. 8″, c. 1910(?).

59. Nestled in the cozy beard of a 1930s Santa mask is a typical 1920s figure of molded cardboard. His wide-set eyes and rather flat face are typical of figures made around this era. German, painted molded cardboard, bottle-brush tree, H. 5½", 1920s.

60. In examining Christmas illustrations and advertisements found in popular literature over the last century, certain trends in holiday decorating become evident. Very noticeable is the heavy interest in sleighs between 1910 and 1930. This Father Christmas-in-a-sleigh figure is both choice and tiny. His facial expression is especially beautiful in so small a piece. The original cost in the 1920s was thirty-five cents. German, composition Santa and reindeer, lead antlers on deer, string reins, mica snow, wooden base, L. 3¾", 1920s.

61. The prominent teeth and smiling face on this joyful Father Christmas make him very special. He is atypical because he wears an original *cotton* beard and carries a *basket*, while he has a plaster over papier-mâché face, which proves once again that there are exceptions to every rule. German, Father Christmas candy container, papier-mâché face, hands, and boots, cotton beard, flannel hood and gown, wooden stick and base, straw basket, H. 10″, c. 1920.

62. A "pointy" beard on this dour Father Christmas allows him great distinction and marks him as one of a variety made with these odd-shaped beards. He was manufactured in several different sizes. Gold mica trim gives him a little holiday sparkle. German, Father Christmas candy container, painted formed cardboard with mica trim, bottle-brush tree (replaced), H. 15½″, 1920s.

63. Since the majority of Santa figures were made to please children, and children love to ski, what could be more natural than a Santa-on-skis? Both the Germans and the Japanese made Santa figures on skis, and later Americans made skiing Santa figures in plastic. German, papier-mâché Santa, rabbit-fur beard, cotton-flannel hat and suit with flannel trim, string belt, cloth sack, cardboard skis with paper baskets, H. 5½", 1920s.

64. Rarely, a figure of Father Christmas is made in this position, bending over his toy pack. Notice how the beard was applied, using adhesive tape, a common practice by old German makers. German, Whitman's candy container, bisque face, fur beard, crepe-paper suit and cap, cotton trim, burlap bag, cardboard base, H. 4½", early 1920s.

65. Saucy candy containers such as these were first manufactured by the Germans during the 1920s. A few years ago they were readily available on the market at almost giveaway prices. Today they show up only occasionally, as people realize their charm. Left to right: all German, 1940–1950, H. 9″, 13″, 8″. Foreground: German Santa candy cornucopia, H. 7″, c. 1920.

66. His face would be enough to persuade even the most truculent children to mend their ways! Santa, pictured here, is a full-length figure and resembles in no small way an angered pagan god. German, Santa, painted mask face, fur beard and hair, "stuffed mitten" hands, rayon suit, fur trim, leather belt and boots, metal buckle, H. 28″, 1920s.

67. A musical Santa from the 1920s is a great find. Turning the key on his back will unleash a jolly rendition of "Jingle Bells." He wears the typical mask face and "stuffed mitten" hands of the 1920s. The creator of this Santa was a sensitive artist. German, Santa, painted buckram mask face, cotton-flannel hands and suit with plush trim, leather belt and boots, metal buckle, H. 26″, 1920s.

47

68. Cross and tired, this Santa has seen many a Christmas since he was made in the 1920s. Originally his body was more rotund; his straw stuffing has shifted downward quite noticeably over the years. Many of the figures from this era have rounded hoods that extend high into the air, as well as mask faces and "stuffed mitten" hands. German, Santa, painted buckram face, fur beard, rayon suit with cotton-flannel trim, leather belt, composition boots, H. 16", 1920s.

69. "On Christmas Day, on Christmas Day, in the morning!" Content that he had done a good job, this fellow was caught about to head up the chimney. His mask face and "stuffed mitten" hands date him as a 1920s figure, and his white fur eyebrows are called "clown's white." German, stuffed Santa, painted buckram mask face, goat-fur beard, rabbit-fur eyebrows, wool suit, leather belt and boots, metal buckle, H. 27", 1920s–1930s.

70. Sporting the typical mask face of Santas made in this era, the "dishrag Santa" here was probably put together by some church member for a Christmas bazaar. His robust health, his bulky overcoat, and his imported buckram face make him irresistible. Probably American, "dishrag Santa," painted buckram face, cotton hair, beard, and undergown, dishrag suit, cotton-ribbon belt, H. 11″, 1920s.

71, 72, 73. "Neither snow, nor rain, nor heat, nor gloom of night stays these couriers from the swift completion of their appointed rounds." Bisque "Immobile Teenies" are a small but significant part of any Santa Claus collection. All German, bisque, 1920s–1930s. Top: Santa on motorcycle, 2¼″ x 3″. Center: Santa pushing cart of goodies, H. 1½″. Bottom: Santa in car, H. 1¼″.

74. Enthusiasts of miniatures especially appreciate the superb molding of these "Immobile Teenies." All German, painted bisque. Left: Father Christmas stuffing a bad boy into his bag, H. 2¼". Center: Father Christmas visiting a child in bed, W. 3". Right: Snowbaby in igloo, Santa above in chimney, H. 2¼", W. 1⅞", 1920–1930s.

75. Italian children love this old witch, especially on Epiphany Eve, January 5! She is *La Befana*, whose name has roots in Epiphany, *Epiphania*. It is she who distributes the Christmas gifts, slipping down chimneys to leave either packages or sticks and stones. Legend has it that shortly after the Christ Child was born, the Three Wise Men passed by her simple cottage on the way to Bethlehem. They asked her to join them in presenting gifts to the Newborn King, but she refused, saying she had little to give. Upon reflection, she convinced herself she did indeed have something to share —an old ragged doll, a ball made of a big seed, some herbs, and a piece of purple cloth, suitable for royalty. But alas! Once she had set out alone on her journey, she could not find her way. Until this day she goes looking into the faces of children, hoping to find the Christ Child. Figures of *La Befana* always carry a broom, because in the legend the old woman was sweeping her cottage when the Wise Men appeared at her door. The figure of the beloved *La Befana* shown here resides in Florence, Italy, and is brought out yearly by her owner, Giuliano Marcantoni, to grace his firm, Pasticceria Maioli, a landmark Florentine coffee bar. She is lifesize and plays a cherished part in the Christmas traditions of both Mr. Marcantoni's family and business. Italian, wax figure with glasses, human-hair wig, broom, regional clothing, H. 5', c. 1920.

76. Soft and romantic, the Père Noël here stands out from all other Father Christmas figures. His delicate pastel coloring and the unique styling of his clothing give immediate proof that he is extraordinary. He does, however, own the typical mask face of the 1920s and 1930s. French, Père Noël candy container, painted mask face, rabbit-fur beard, cotton-wadding suit with gold mica trim, papier-mâché boots; marked "La Riviera, Nice 8006, 184 E," late 1920s–early 1930s, H. 14″.

# 1930-1940

77. This is not the usual Santa Claus costume. As early as 1854, he appeared in a *Harper's Weekly* drawing dressed in this manner—a short coat over fitted pants and tight boots. Another illustration in 1912 showed him dressed in identical fashion. Here he is in 1930. His torso is a candy container that lifts off to reveal the candy cylinder. German, Santa candy container, papier-mâché face, hands, and legs, dog-fur beard (replaced), cloth suit, leather boots, bottle-brush tree (replaced), H. 8″, 1930s.

78. Properly described as an advertising item, this Buster Brown giveaway was a highly prized gift in the Depression of the early 1930s. Founded in 1904 when the Brown Shoe Company purchased the rights to the *Buster Brown* comic strips, the company over the years has handed out hundreds of appealing premiums to young customers. Other American shoe companies cottoned to the idea, and various Santa figures are available labeled in a similar manner but with different company names. German, painted formed cardboard, twigs in hand, H. 6½″, early 1930s.

79. Relatives meet to exchange Season's Greetings! Both belong to the Steiff family, toymakers since before the turn of the century and originators of America's captivating Teddy Bear. The old clown is a key-wind toy that can walk. German, Santa, rubber face, synthetic beard, flannel suit, boots of rayon and wool, cotton trim, felt hands, H. 13½", late 1930s–early 1940s.

80. In spite of his broken ceramic robe, this incense burner Santa is infinitely appealing and collectible. Like German wooden "smokers," his mouth is open, all the better to enjoy the aroma of the burning incense. German, painted ceramic, H. 3½", c. 1930.

81. This little Santa is very interesting because he is French and because he so closely resembles a French doll known as "Minerve." A contemporary Minerve doll is pictured below; such dolls are still available today in France. French, all-paper Santa, cotton beard, push-pin nose, H. 2½″, 1930s–1940s.

82. Although this figure looks like a doll masquerading as Father Christmas, it is really a candy container. It cannot be positively identified as either German or Japanese in origin, but the roughness of the bisque, the reddish skin tones, the arresting blue eyes, and the use of Japanese materials —cotton in the beard, crepe and tissue paper in the hat and bag—all point to Japanese manufacture. German or Japanese, Father Christmas candy container, bisque face and hands, glass eyes, cotton beard, satin gown with flannel trim, crepe-paper hat, tissue-paper bag, H. 9″, late 1920s–early 1930s.

83. The Germans made many Santas-in-sleighs. Most Santas were papier-mâché figures in either cardboard or log sleighs. The rare figure here, on the right, is made of painted wax that was first molded. Both German, Santas-in-sleighs. Left: painted papier-mâché face, cotton beard (replaced), flannel suit, paper belt, L. 3″; cardboard sleigh with white sand finish, 4½″, hooks for reindeer, c. 1930. Right: painted wax face, beard, and boots, colored cotton-wadding suit painted with "snow," goose-feather tree, wooden sled, H. 5½″; Santa, H. 3½″, c. 1935.

84. Miniaturists would love this Santa-in-a-sleigh. The entire set measures not more than two inches long! Still, the detailing is clear, and the features expressive. Delightful! Japanese, all Celluloid Santa-in-a-sleigh with reindeer, L. 2″, 1930s.

85. In step with the American interest in Santas-in-sleighs during this period, Japanese makers turned them out by the hundreds. The deer were Celluloid; the sleighs, painted cardboard. Cheap and colorful, they sold exceedingly well in the United States. Japanese, Santa, clay face, hands, and boots, cotton beard, flannel suit and trim, bottle-brush tree, Celluloid deer, painted wooden base, 6″ x 9¼″, 1930s.

86. At first glance this graceless Santa looks Aleut (perhaps because he is standing on ice floes), but he is most likely Japanese in origin. His flat facial structure, orangish skin tones, and the use of maribou as trim on his coat all suggest Japanese manufacture. Japanese, Santa, clay face, cotton beard, flannel jacket, cotton pants, maribou trim on hood and coat, paper boots, rayon bag, H. 16″, 1940s–1950s.

87. On his way from the North Pole! Awkward and enchanting, the Japanese manage to capture a certain casual charm lacking in more meticulous renditions of these favorite Christmas figures. Japanese, Santa, papier-mâché face, hands, and boots, felt suit, rabbit-fur beard (replaced), paper belt, H. 3″; paper reindeer with wire and ribbon harness, painted cardboard sleigh, L. 8″, 1930s.

88. It is less common to find a Japanese Santa in a cotton-wadding suit, as seen here, than in a flannel one. And not many Japanese Santas carry a walking stick. Japanese, Santa on a candy box, clay face and boots, cotton-wadding hood and suit with flannel trim, wooden staff, cotton cloth bag, *Erika-moos* greens, composition berries, painted cardboard box with mica trim, H. 6″, 1930s.

89. Three versions of the basic Japanese Santa are available to the novice collector at reasonable prices. Their innate charm, however, should not be underestimated. All Japanese, Santas, cotton beards and cotton-flannel suits, 1930s. Left: clay face and feet, cardboard base, holding kugel, H. 6″. Center: clay face and feet, cardboard base, holding bottle-brush tree, H. 6″. Right: Celluloid face, clay feet, cardboard base, holding bottle-brush tree and net bag, H. 6″.

90. Among the seemingly infinite variety of Japanese Santas is this one in an all-chenille suit. Chenille is usually reserved for trim. Japanese, Santa, clay face and hands, cotton beard, chenille cap, body, and boots, paper belt, fabric sack, cardboard stand, H. 8″, 1930s.

91. *Bizarre* is the only word to describe this amazing Japanese Santa Claus. His high color is outrageous and guaranteed to set teeth on edge. Yet there is no collector who would pass him by! Japanese, Santa, composition face and hands, cotton beard, flannel suit with fur trim, paper belt and buckle, cotton cloth bag, wooden walking stick, H. 10″, 1930s.

92. Pine cone Christmas men were handmade beginning in 1868. These pictured are all Japanese, made in the 1930s. The·Santa on the right is similar to the French one in plate 81, but the little Père Noël has more style and quality. Craftsmen of today could easily fashion Santa figures of cones such as these. All Japanese, pine cone Santas, 1930s. Left: pressed-cardboard face, cotton beard, chenille arms and trim, cardboard disk feet, H. 3½". Center: clay face, flannel cap, chenille trim, *Erikamoos* tree, log base, H. 5½". Right: paper-covered, painted wood ball head, flannel cap, chenille trim, net bag, paper feet, H. 3".

93. The Santa battalion "at the ready" here is but a small part of those made of Celluloid. America produced fine Celluloid figures, as did Germany and Japan. Left to right, late 1920s–early 1940s: 1. Japanese, H. 4½". 2. American, the Irwin Company, H. 6". 3. American, the Irwin Company, H. 3". 4. American, the Irwin Company, H. 7". 5. American, the Irwin Company, H. 4". 6. American, marked U S A, H. 5". 7. American, marked "Made in U.S.A.," H. 4¼".

94. The Japanese version of the old German roly-poly toy. Japanese, roly-poly Santa-on-a-ball, painted Celluloid, H. 4½", 1930s.

95. Fifteen cents could buy this happy Santa-on-a-train baby rattle in 1930. The careful detailing is unusual on an inexpensive Japanese piece. Japanese, Celluloid, H. 5½", 1930s.

96. A singular figure, this Japanese Santa is a "rocker." His head rests on a clockwork pendulum device in the back. When perfectly balanced, a tiny nudge will enable him to "tick-tock" for about five minutes. His detailed molding is exemplary. Japanese, Celluloid "rocker" Santa, tin base, H. 7¾", 1930s.

97. In the 1930s it was popular to place electric candles or electrified glass Santa bulbs on mantels as decoration. They were also placed on windowsills to greet passersby. This tradition had roots in an old belief that the Christ Child, seeing a light in a window, might stop for shelter and comfort. The Santas originally stood in Bakelite bases seen here. Behind them is a painted Christmas tree stand from the same period. These are but two varieties of large Santa light bulbs of the many produced during this time. Japanese, molded-glass Santa Claus bulbs, 1930s. Left: H. 5½". Right: H. 9".

98, 99. In the 1930s the Japanese mass-produced inexpensive cardboard cottages, houses, and churches (often covered with white flocking). When a sufficient number were used together, it was possible to make very effective village scenes, which were charming by themselves or under the Christmas tree. Often a Santa would be placed in front of a building, as seen here. Occasionally a building would have a hole in the back where a light could be inserted for nighttime glow. Or sometimes a series of houses was used on the Christmas tree over a string of lights. Both Japanese, cardboard cottages with cardboard bases. Top: candy container, Santa with clay face, flannel suit, chenille trim, added glitter, H. 5½", 1930s. Bottom: clay Santa, corrugated paper fence, sponge trees, H. 2½", 1930s.

100. Santa traveling in an airship appears as early as 1910 in a Christmas illustration from *St. Nicholas Magazine.* Thereafter he navigated in air machines quite regularly until they faded from the scene in the 1930s. German glassblowers made ornaments of Santas riding in air gondolas after the turn of the century; these were crudely copied in other media by the Japanese in the 1920s, as seen here. Nonetheless, this imaginative Santa candy container is greatly prized. Japanese, Santa candy container, cotton-wadding suit and cap, chenille trim, cotton beard, cardboard gondola and canopy, base to top H. 4½″; gondola L. 5″, late 1920s.

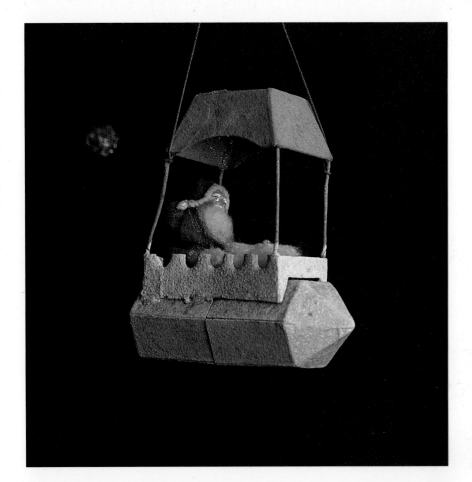

101. Illustrations featuring Santas in airplanes appeared in American magazines during the first decade of the twentieth century after the Wright Brothers' historic flight in 1903. By the time the Japanese made this figure, airplanes were commonplace, but the Santas-in-airplanes were some of the most whimsical ever created. Japanese, Santa, clay face, cotton beard, cotton suit with chenille trim; torso and head H. 1¼″; cardboard and glitter airplane, L. 5½″, 1920s–1930s.

102. A Japanese approach to an old standby, this chenille boot is meant to hold candy and hang from a tree branch. After the war the United States turned out millions of plastic ones. Japanese, Santa, clay face, cotton-flannel hood, cotton hands, chenille-covered cardboard boot, paper ribbon trim and hanger, H. 8½", 1930s.

103. Another version of a favorite, the boot candy container. Japanese, foil-covered boot with chenille trim, Santa with clay face, cotton beard, cotton suit, net bag, H. 6½", 1930s.

104. Drawing on the old European concept of Santa Claus leaving gifts in children's shoes, the Japanese conceived this attractive candy bag that, when filled with goodies, was hung on the tree for well-behaved children. Japanese, Celluloid Santa face and hands, cotton-flannel hood and robe with chenille trim, flannel boot, cotton mesh bag with drawstrings, silver paper leaves, 5″ x 7″, 1930s.

105. The Santa-in-a-basket pictured here is another variation of the popular Japanese candy bag. Cotton mesh is more commonly used than flannel for the candy sack, but either kind does the job well enough! Japanese, Santa candy container, Celluloid face and hands, cotton-flannel body, sack with drawstrings, woven straw basket, H. 4½″, 1930s.

106. A gathering of the clan—three Japanese candy-bag Santas, all basically the same—provides "variations on a theme." Note the subtle differences in facial expression and the use of different but similar fabrics. In all three, heavy clay feet act as ballast for the hanging figures. All Japanese, 1930s. Left: Celluloid face, clay hands and feet, flannel cap with lace trim, felt buttons, fine net bag, H. 6½″. Center: Celluloid face and hands, cotton-flannel suit with glass buttons, clay feet, coarse net bag, H. 7½″. Right: Celluloid face, clay hands and feet, cotton-flannel suit with chenille trim, silver-paper star buttons, coarse net bag, H. 8″.

107, 108, 109. These three Japanese "hanger" Santas elicit many adjectives—fanciful, far-fetched, weird, charming—eccentric. There were a variety of them on the market in the 1930s, all illustrating the inventiveness of the Japanese mind. They were made primarily for the American trade. Three "hanger" Japanese Santas. 107. Top: Santa bell, clay face, cotton beard, chenille body, bell, and tree, glass ball ornamentation, H. 10½", 1930s. 108. Center: 3 wreaths of papier mâché with paper chenille ropes, foil-covered suit with clay face, cotton beard, chenille trim, flannel legs, chenille tree, Santa, H. 4", overall H. 13", 1930s. 109. Bottom: clay face, hands, and feet, fur beard (replaced), net body bag, paper hat, arms, and candy box, H. 5", 1930s.

69

110. Santa-in-the-round: a potpourri of gift givers makes a splendid wreath! See line drawing below for identification. 1. Japanese milk-glass light bulb, H. 3½", 1930s. 2. German bisque torso with feather tree, H. 3¼", 1910. 3. American "Keepsake Egg," scrap Santa head, H. 2½", 1981. 4. Norman Rockwell Santa, H. 3½", 1982. 5. Japanese red chenille Santa with clay face, H. 3¼", 1930s. 6. Japanese green chenille Santa with clay face, H. 3¼", 1930s. 7. American Santa with composition face, fabric hat, H. 6", 1940s–1950s. 8. German blown-glass Santa tree ornament, H. 7", c. 1890. 9. Ecuadoran woven-straw Santa candy box, H. 4¼", 1970s. 10. Japanese milk-glass light bulb, H. 3", 1930s. 11. Japanese Santa with glass head, googly eyes, H. 3¼", 1950s. 12. German painted plaster Father Christmas, H. 5½", 1981. 13. American Santa Claus light, H. 3", 1920s. 14. German painted lead Santa, H. 2", 1950s. 15. German plaster Father Christmas, H. 3", 1920s. 16. Japanese milk-glass bulb, missing paint, H. 2¼", 1930s. 17. Taiwanese plastic Father Christmas, H. 6½", 1977. 18. Japanese milk-glass light bulb, H. 3", 1930s. 19. Japanese bisque Santa, H. 4", 1930s. 20. Japanese cotton-wadding Santa torso, H. 5", 1930s. 21. Japanese milk-glass light bulb, two-sided, H. 3", 1930s. 22. Flannel-suited Occupied Japan Santa, H. 3", 1940s. 23. Candy-cookie Father Christmas, St. Louis, Missouri, H. 4", 1975. 24. "Teeny" Japanese bisque Santa, H. 1¾", 1930s. 25. Early Hallmark stuffed Santa, cotton, H. 6", 1970s.

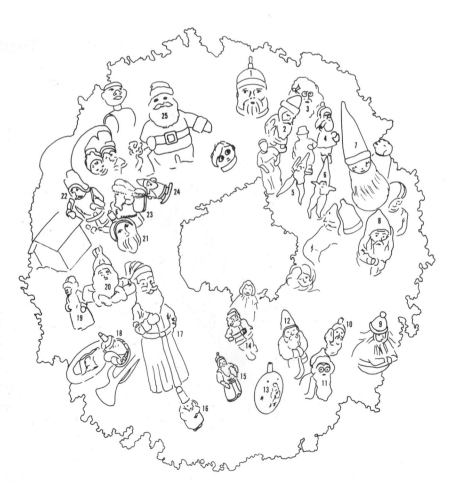

111. As pedestrian as this Christmas vignette is, it is important only because it is a part of the 1920–1930 era and because it illustrates how some of the pressed-cardboard figures were incorporated into Christmas "scenes." Probably American, Santa and fireplace scene, painted and finished with mica, made of chip board, 10″ x 14½″ x 7¼″. Santa, H. 4¼″. Bottle-brush tree, wooden logs with *Erikamoos* and ribbons, 1920–1930.

112. These jolly gentlemen were purchased from a man whose father had used them for Christmas candy displays in a rural town in eastern Washington during the 1930s. They were available until the early 1950s. Composed of pressed cardboard, the material resembles that found in old egg cartons. More like the Santas of today, the figures have become shorter and stouter than their predecessors. The Santa-in-the-sleigh has been lacquered before being painted. All American, pressed cardboard, 1930s–1950s. Left to right: 1. Santa, H. 6¾″, sleigh and pack H. 7½″. 2. Santa with front pack, H. 11″. 3. Santa with mica-covered pack, H. 9″. 4. Santa, no pack, H. 9¾″.

113. Crudely painted and originally not costly, this old Father Christmas candy container, filled with red-hots, has a metal closure as a base. Earlier ones were corked. The manufacturer's logo is pressed into the tin base. The candy weighs one ounce. Glass candy containers became exceedingly popular during Victorian times and remained so for decades. American, painted pressed-glass Father Christmas candy container, with screw-type tin base, logo in base reads $\mathbb{V}$, H. 5¼", 1930s.

114. A Father Christmas figure holding a saber is both strange and rare. Charles Dickens alludes to it in his famous *Christmas Carol* (1843). He describes Old Father Christmas this way: "Girded around [his] middle was an antique scabbard; but no sword was in it, and the ancient sheath was eaten up with rust." Undoubtedly the saber was a vestige from early pagan days. The lithographed figure here supports a full-length candy sack on his back. Probably American, all-paper Father Christmas candy container, H. 9", date unknown.

72

115. This patented "walk-man" Santa of the late 1930s was invented by Ned F. Wagner and John E. Wilson of Watsonville, Pennsylvania. Their patent number, 2,140,275, was registered by the U.S. Patent Office in the *Official Gazette* on December 13, 1938. A technical description found in the *Gazette* relates how the curved foot tread, the convergent legs, and the conical body allow the figure to take regular steps down a slight incline. American, composition face, beard, and cap, cotton-flannel suit and trim over basic cardboard cone, wooden hands and feet, patent number on right foot, H. 5½″, 1938.

116. Very tall and eye-catching, this Santa promoted Christmas cards from Gibson Greeting Cards, Inc., located in Cincinnati, Ohio. American, printed cardboard standup Santa, H. 30″, E. J. King, artist, probably 1940s.

117. The label on this figure, "Made in Germany, U.S. Occupied Zone," clearly dates its manufacture between July 1945 and September 1949. Allowing for a period of "tooling up," the actual time in which the piece could have been made was very short. It cannot help being a comparative rarity as it was in production for such a brief time, and furthermore it is an extremely handsome piece. German, U.S. Occupied Zone. Santa: wire armature, clay head, feet, and hands, flannel suit, artificial fur trim, H. 7″. Reindeer: artificial-fur coat, oilcloth harness, glass eyes, composition feet (antlers missing), L. 8″. Sleigh: painted wood, braided wool, and green sponge trim, L. 12″, 1945–1949.

118. Proof that Germany continued to export handsome Christmas items after the war, even if supplies were limited. Felt faces, seen on Kathe Kruse and Lenci dolls, were used on Santas, too, as seen here. West German, Santa in paper-covered box, H. 4¾″, felt face and hands, cotton beard, flannel suit and hood, terrycloth trim, silver bell rings; figure extends 3½″ above rim of box when open, post–World War II.

119. The passing of Old World craftsmanship is already noticeable on this postwar Father Christmas. While his face is molded, it lacks the fine detail of earlier models. The facial features were now airbrushed on, not painstakingly hand painted. The figure is attractive and pleasing, but certainly not top drawer. German, Father Christmas, papier-mâché face and hands, rabbit-fur beard, flannel suit and trim, string belt, formed cardboard boots, H. 8″, post–World War II.

120. Santa Claus and Coca-Cola were well acquainted long before this midcentury figure was made. This Santa, pouring from the familiar bottle, is highly collectible albeit of recent manufacture. American, Santa, plastic face and hands, cotton-plush suit with plush trim, vinyl belt and boots, H. 17″, 1950s–1960s.

121. Advertising a popular watch of the 1950s, this Santa Claus was undoubtedly used in a jewelry store as a display piece. American, Santa, plastic face, belt, and boots, manmade carded "wool" beard, velvet suit and trim, H. 16″, 1950s.

122. This particular 1950s Santa was also available without advertising material. Here he is, busy at his old Eagle stove, cooking up some goodies to take along in his pack! American, Santa, plastic face, belt, and boots, manmade carded "wool" beard, velvet suit and trim, H. 16″, 1950s.

123. Never to be overlooked are Santas made by loving hands at home. Here is a handmade fellow put together by a mother or grandmother for some eager child. Santas were printed onto cotton patterns meant to be cut out and stitched as early as 1911. The Louis Lindner and Sons Company made a handsome Father Christmas pattern; the printed figure held a tree in one hand and a basket of goodies in the other. Later, from 1913 until 1923, the Art Fabric Mills company in Newark, New Jersey, produced dolls and a few Santas, printed on muslin, ready to be worked and stuffed. Probably American, stuffed cotton Santa, embroidered features, cotton suit with chenille trim, gold-foil belt buckle, H. 13″, 1950s.

124. Half-gnome, half-Santa, this strange fellow holding two children is built over a wire armature. His weird, oversize hands are formed of wrapped paper over wire. The children's shoes are particularly curious. Probably American, composition face and feet, wrapped paper over wire hands, wire body, crepe-paper and cloth suit, H. 6", c. 1950.

125. Cast-iron banks (with a firm's name and address) were excellent giveaways and savings incentives for both children and adults. This one, a fine piece of cast iron, was a gift from the Security Savings and Loan Company of Aberdeen, Washington. American, painted cast-iron still bank, plaque on side contains legend, H. 4", post–World War II.

126. Postwar Santa figures from Japan were cheaply made, lacking the great appeal of those from the 1920s and 1930s. Because their trousers were made of rolled paper, they stand in a very stiff fashion and have a tendency to lean forward. All Japanese, Santas, cotton beards, flannel suits and hoods, chenille trim, pipe-cleaner hands and feet, cardboard bases, 1950s–1960s. Left: plastic face, H. 6″, with paper candle. Center: cardboard face, H. 5″, bottle-brush tree. Right: cardboard face, H. 5″, bottle-brush tree branch.

127. Another version of a favorite toy, this Santa-in-a-chimney is entrancing even though he was made fairly recently. Unlike many, the chimney has no top, and Santa bobs up and down inside it. Japanese, Santa-in-a-chimney, rubber head and body, chromolithographed tin chimney (H. 5″), key windup, 1950s.

128, 129. Commonly for sale in flea markets, these two tin and plastic windups are among the least expensive Santa figures. Both "ding" as they move along. Although not premium items for Christmas collectors, they are fun to own. Toy collectors show increasing interest in the newer Japanese mechanical tin toys. Both Japanese. Top: Santa-in-a-sleigh with reindeer, H. 3½″, metal bell and key-wind base, L. 4½″, rayon cord reins, 1950–1960s. Bottom: Santa-on-motorcycle, all Celluloid except for cycle frame, metal bell, rubber wheels, H. 4″, 1950s–1960s.

130. In 1939 cartoonist Max Fleischner presented Earth with a superbeing, a refugee from the planet Krypton. As reported in *Superman Magazine,* Superman, alias Clark Kent, was discovered in an orphanage and raised by his adoptive parents, Jonathan and Martha Kent. Champion of the oppressed, Superman has remained a superhuman favorite of many people. In the late 1960s his popularity again soared. It is doubtful that this SuperSanta from that era could perform Tarzan-like deeds, but he plays a super role in the whole super Santa scene. Japanese, the Kamar Company, cotton felt, plastic face, H. 6½", 1967.

131, 132. Many battery-operated Santa Claus figures appeared in the 1950s and 1960s; these are eagerly collected by toy and Christmas buffs alike. The one at the top has eyes that light up intermittently while he simultaneously moves his hand up and down to ring his Christmas bell. The Santa at the bottom rings his bell as he rotates on the world globe. Many other varieties exist —some walk and others can even turn the metallic pages of a Christmas songbook using magnets on their hands—and batteries! Both American, lithographed tin, battery-operated Santas. Top: Noël Decorations, Inc., switch-controlled, vinyl face, cotton beard, rayon velvet suit with fake-fur trim, metal bell, plastic boots; H. of figure 8″, overall H. 11″, copyright 1960. Bottom: vinyl face, cotton whiskers, cotton-velvet suit and cap with plush trim, vinyl boots, metal bell and world globe base, H. 15″, 1950s–1960s.

133. Gifts are brought to Italian children by the Christ Child, the *Gesù Bambino,* on January 6, Feast of the Epiphany. But Italian children are not unfamiliar with *Babbo Natale,* who resembles Father Christmas more than the American Santa Claus. Traditionally, he is a friendly old man with a long white beard who exists in the minds of Italian children and who, if they're good, might make one quick appearance on Christmas morning. Italian, painted papier-mâché figure with cloth bag of fresh greens, wooden base, H. 10″, 1977.

134. These odd Christmas fellows are unique to Spain. Made of short lengths of logs, the legs are smaller twigs cut to size. Facial features are cut pieces of red, black, and white felt glued onto the cut ends of the logs. They all sport cheery red caps and are the closest facsimiles of Santa Claus figures in Spain. Spanish, Santa Claus figures of wood, trimmed in felt, various sizes, 1982–1983.

135. Purchased in Salzburg, Austria, this plastic Father Christmas is quite winsome in spite of being a product of the synthetic age. He once carried a bag of Mozartkugeln in his backpack. He stands near a wreath from Salzburg; dried flower work is one of Austria's most illustrious crafts. Austrian, painted plastic Father Christmas, orlon beard, suit, and trim, artificial tree, painted cardboard base, mica-covered, H. 7½″, 1983.

136. Home office for Lanz apparel and fabrics is Salzburg, Austria. Known worldwide for its quality Tyrolean merchandise, Lanz goods are held in high esteem by young and old. Each year the company produces a Santa Claus incorporating its fabrics into various designs. Seen here is the 1981 Santa, photographed at the home office in Salzburg. Lanz makes tree ornaments for sale in Austria, but this Santa was for display only. Austrian, Santa, all wool except for wooden staff with glass ornament top, beaded muffler, H. 6″, 1981.

137. A short visit to Budapest in December 1981 failed to turn up many signs of Christmas except for a few street vendors peddling plastic Santa Claus candy containers, strings of lights, packages of tinsel, and some glass ball ornaments. The communist satellite was observing life as usual. This fearsome fellow, however, carved by a Hungarian for export trade, is a real find and conveys especially well the wisdom of philanthropy throughout the year. Hungarian, carved wooden face, hemp beard, molded composition hands and feet, wool-flannel suit and hood, burlap bag, wooden staff, H. 6½″, 1980.

138. This striking contemporary Father Christmas face is actually a hand puppet from Dresden. It is one of a series that includes witches, clowns, fairies, and dolls. He is widely sold in toy stores and mail-order catalogues. East German, painted cotton felt with plush trim, burlap sack, real sticks; made by Künstlerpuppe, H. 13½″, 1981–1983.

139. As in many Latin countries, Mexican Christmas festivities center on the *pesebre,* the Nativity. Gifts are distributed on the Feast of the Epiphany, January 6, and Santa Claus plays no real role in their celebrations. The figure pictured here was handcrafted for the tourist trade. He can also be purchased riding on a bicycle or pushing a wheelbarrow. Bright, joyous colors distinguish Mexican crafts. Mexican, Santa, lacquered tin, 8″ x 9½″, 1980.

140. This Santa Claus from El Salvador displays a great similarity to the clay Nativity figures from Mexico. Both countries love bright colors and use wired clay balls (here ornaments on the Christmas tree) for heightened effect. The detail is marvelous on such a small piece. El Salvadoran, Santa, painted clay, wire armature, H. 2″, 1980s.

141, 142. Here are two versions of *Jultomten,* the Swedish gift giver who arrives after the traditional smorgasbord on Christmas Eve, accompanied by *Julbock,* the goat of straw. Top: Swedish *Jultomten,* molded Sculpey face, hands, and feet, flannel suit and cap, burlap bag, H. 9½″, 1980. Bottom: Swedish, *Jultomten,* vinyl face, hands, legs, and boots, nylon beard, hand-knit wool cap, sweater, and stockings, H. 15″, 1981.

143. Handcarved from one piece of wood (except for the applied beard), then painted, this stylistic *Jultomten* from Sweden exemplifies superior Scandinavian design. It is odd that the facial features are merely inked in with a felt-tip pen, as it is a fairly expensive piece. Swedish, *Jultomten,* all painted, carved wood except for inked face, H. 8″, 1981.

144. From the land of Hans Christian Andersen comes this impish *Julnisse* who lives in the lofts of farmhouses and is the source of many practical jokes in Danish households. The *Julnisse* is kin to Sweden's *Jultomten* and Norway's *Julesvenn.* Danish, *Julnisse,* hemp body, wood face, knitted wool cap, fur beard, H. 10″, 1981.

145. Current Taiwanese Santa Claus figures offer a wide selection in bisque. Many American companies hire artists to design figures that are then fabricated in Taiwan. All Taiwanese painted bisque. Left: Playing Santa Claus, by Enesco Import Co., H. 6½", 1983. Center: Santa roly-poly with hanger, stuffed body, wool clothes, plastic belt and buttons, H. 6", designed by Linda Massopust for Dept. 56, 1983. Right: Father Christmas with hanger, H. 4½", 1983.

146. Considered the Spirit of Winter, this Grandfather Frost (*Ded Moroz*) is appropriately costumed. He was one of two sent to the author by an Intourist guide in Leningrad; the other figure was identical except for its red suit and hat. Maria, the guide, received permission from her superiors to ship them when they learned they were to be used for educational purposes. Russian, Grandfather Frost, painted composition face, blue satin coat, pink satin domed hat, pressed-cotton beard, mittens, and trim, wooden staff and base, H. 20", 1979.

147. This Grandfather Frost, which turned up at a Christmas market in Zurich, Switzerland, shares many characteristics with blown-glass tree ornaments exported to America during the same period. The turbanlike hat and treated cotton beard are clues useful in identifying Russian figures. His gray robe is very appealing, but the whole figure is so tenuously held together that it is not pleasurable to handle it. Russian, Grandfather Frost, painted plastic face (peeling), "sealed" cotton beard, paper skirt with cotton-wadding trim over pink plastic body and feet, plastic tree and wooden stick, H. 12″, 1982.

148. Another Grandfather Frost from Russia is startlingly beautiful in spite of his being plastic. His delicate coloring and molding make him magical. He was purchased in Russia. Russian, Grandfather Frost, painted plastic, some areas treated with a luster finish, H. 14″, 1978.

91

149. All three of these Santas from today's craftsmen are available in stores. In the basket, left, is a velvet soft sculpture that sold in great numbers throughout the United States. In the center is the much-fancied Troll Santa so in demand during the 1960s. He appeared in many different guises. On the right is the new German Steiff Santa, *Knopf im Ohr*, "with the button in the ear." The little metal button is the company trademark. Although not as exciting to own as others, these three still have a place in anyone's collection—or heart! Left: American, Santa, stuffed cotton velvet and flannel, by My Favorite Things, Carmel, California, H. 24″, 1970s–1980s. Center: Probably American, Troll Santa, glass eyes, plastic, animal fur, H. 10″, 1960s. Right: West German, Steiff Santa, plastic face, metal glasses, velvet suit, synthetic fur, vinyl boots and belt, H. 12″, 1980s.

150. Few can resist this capricious creature taking a time-out from his strenuous rounds. A contemporary Santa, he proves again that it is not necessary to be old to be desirable! American, Santa, handmade of felt and cotton, painted features, mink-fur trim, metal eyeglasses, H. 22″, 1970s.

151. A Father Christmas under a dome can be a handsome, simple addition to Christmas festivities. American, painted plaster Father Christmas, glass dome, wooden base with statice, painted Andromeda pods, and wrapped packages; H. of dome 8″, 1982.

152. Standing in front of an impressive Crazy patchwork quilt dated 1883, this contemporary Father Christmas might almost pass for the real thing. His features are delicately molded and painted bisque, but the bisque is not as fine-grained or as realistically tinted as its antique prototypes. He is, nevertheless, a splendid figure, made by Faith Wick of Grand Rapids, Michigan. American, Father Christmas, bisque face and hands, synthetic beard and hair, cloth body, nylon suit with fake-fur trim, leather belt, H. 20″, 1979.

153. Fresh from his box, this Father Christmas is quite bare. Exposure to the air for twenty-four hours, however, will transform him into a Pelze-Nicol of olden days. He is made of soap and is hygroscopic. A favorite toy from the past that has recently been revived, he remains a lure for recalcitrant children at the sink or in the bathtub. They still thrill at watching him grow his luxuriant white coat! American, Father Christmas, soap with painted face and trim, H. 4¼″, 1970s–1980s.

154. Hallmark Cards, Inc., has been producing a Christmas ornament line for the last few years. Traditionally, at least a few of these are Santa Claus figures. The ornaments are noteworthy because of their excellent craftsmanship, creativity, and modest prices. This is a tin ornament from the 1981 offering. Another model, a lithographed tin Santa Claus available in 1983, is unique because it has articulated limbs. Some of these Santas will be the treasures of tomorrow. American, lithographed tin Santa, H. 4¼″, 1981.

155. In the 1970s interest in collecting old tins reached its zenith. This roly-poly Santa tobacco tin is a reproduction of an old one and continues to be a great commercial success in the 1980s. American, lithographed tin Santa, made by Bristol Ware of Chein Industries, H. 7″, 1980.

156. Modeled after the traditional Father Christmas of the 1890s, this simple figure of basswood represents an Oregon wood-carver's first attempt at figure making. Glenn R. Day chose to use basswood because it is "butter-soft and shows no grain." American, Father Christmas, wood, H. 9″, 1978.

157. Annalee Thorndike is a designer-dollmaker who makes flexible felt Santa Claus figures with hand-painted faces. Their impish personality quickly caught on, and the Annalee Mobilitee dolls have been and continue to be huge commercial successes. They are one of America's best-known Christmas figures. The company is located in Meredith, New Hampshire. American, Santa Claus, machine-painted felt face, wire armature frame, synthetic beard, velour suit, H. 4', 1984.

158. Over a hundred years ago the drawing for this superlative Father Christmas appeared in *Godey's Lady's Book.* The original featured a papier-mâché face, hands, and boots. It takes the artist, Susan Shroyer, four hours to apply the flax beard, piece by piece. The maker of other Christmas figures, she annually decorates an authentic Victorian tree for the Wing House Museum in Coldwater, Michigan. American, Father Christmas, plaster face, hands, and boots, flax beard, pine cone arms, body, and legs, wool muffler, bottle-brush tree, mole-fur cap, antique materials in toys, switches, wooden base, H. 15″, 1983.

159. This rear view of the pine cone Father Christmas illustrated above shows the fantastic toys he carries in his pack, copies of those seen in Thomas Nast illustrations, a Marshall Field Christmas catalogue of 1891–1892, and actual toys dating from this period. The Santa-in-a-box is on a minuscule spring and bobs merrily about. Each candy stick and licorice whip is formed gently by hand.

160. Contemporary Father Christmas figures can be magnificent, too. The artist is Gladys Lang, from the Midwest. Of special merit are the sculptured face, the gloved hands, the marcelled beard, and the delightful tarlatan bag of Christmas goodies. American, Father Christmas, by Gladys Lang, Sculpey face, hands, and boots, synthetic treated beard, velvet suit, fur trim, bottle-brush tree, burlap sack, tarlatan stocking, wooden base, H. 14″, 1982.

# APPRAISAL GUIDE

This Appraisal Guide has been compiled on the basis of values set in 1984 for St. Nicholas, Father Christmas, and Santa Claus figures. It reflects the judgment of knowledgeable collectors from different regions of the United States. Values are given on the assumption that a Christmas figure is in prime condition. If a figure has been damaged in any way or if any parts are missing, this fact has been noted and a lower appraisal has been determined. Naturally it is impossible to include all the Christmas figures that exist today, but with careful reasoning, in most cases it will be possible to extrapolate from the facts included here and come up with a reasonable assessment for an unlisted figure. General appeal, age, condition, and scarcity are all important in trying to determine value. Unfortunately in the last few years, values have been rising at a fast pace, and no relief seems in sight as more and more people discover the attraction of Christmas items, particularly Christmas figures.

| | | |
|---|---|---:|
| | Frontispiece Père Noël of painted, molded cardboard; French | $ 800 |
| 1 | Mechanical Father Christmas with puppet-on-string music box; German | 1,700 |
| 2 | Early Father Christmas, wood with flannel suit; German | 175–200 |
| 3 | Father Christmas in tin sleigh; pulled by goats, mechanical; German | 2,000+ |
| 4 | Bisque-faced Father Christmas in paper suit; German* | 300 |
| 5 | Early cotton-wadding Father Christmas, papier-mâché face, basket; German | 500–600 |
| 6 | Papier-mâché Father Christmas, small, white; German | 100–125 |
| 7 | Papier-mâché Father Christmas, white, red hood; German | $ 275 |
| 8 | Papier-mâché Father Christmas, very tall, white; German* | 1,500 |
| 9 | Papier-mâché Father Christmas, holly wreath on hood; German | 500–550 |
| 10 | Plaster over papier-mâché Father Christmas, green suit; German | 250–275 |
| 11 | Plaster over papier-mâché Father Christmas, lavender suit; German* | 250 |
| 12 | Plaster over papier-mâché Father Christmas, gold suit; German | 450 |
| 13 | Plaster over papier-mâché Father Christmas, flannel suit; German | 400–500 |
| 14 | Plaster over papier-mâché Father | |

*Figure is a candy container.

Christmas, flannel-trimmed cap; German $ 300

15 Plaster over papier-mâché Father Christmas, velvet suit; German 350

16 Plaster over papier-mâché Father Christmas with basket; German 450–500

17 Plaster over papier-mâché Father Christmas torso; German 400

18 Papier-mâché Father Christmas, floor-length robe, lantern; German* 800

19 Papier-mâché Father Christmas in sleigh, pull-toy base; German 1,200

20 Papier-mâché Pelze-Nicol, flannel suit; German 175

21 Papier-mâché Pelze-Nicol, fur coat; German 500

22 Father Christmas, scrap face, crepe-paper suit; German 75

23 Plaster over papier-mâché Father Christmas, mohair coat; German 600

24 Plaster over papier-mâché Father Christmas, plush coat; German 150–175

25 Cotton-wadding Father Christmas, scrap face; German 150

26 Left: cotton-wadding Father Christmas, scrap face; German 100

Right: cotton-wadding Father Christmas, scrap face; German 75–85

27 Painted pressed-cardboard Father Christmas; German 15–65

28 Die-cut chromolithographed Father Christmas; German 175–200

29 Papier-mâché roly-poly Father Christmas, weighted; German 150

30 Tin chocolate molds of Father Christmas, St. Nicholas; German, American 25–100

31 *Eierzucken* (egg sugar) Father Christmas; German 35–40

32 Tin Santa Claus cookie cutters; German 8–25

33 Painted gourd Santa; origin unknown 35–40

34 Painted cast-iron Santa-at-chimney mechanical bank; American good 350 very good 525 mint 675

35 Blown-glass Santa Claus and Father Christmas ornaments; German 20–75

36 Spun-glass Father Christmas, scrap face; German 45–50

37 Spun-glass Father Christmas, wax head; German 175–200

38 Father Christmas nodder, iron hands;

German $ 550–600

39 Plaster St. Nicholas, fabric robes; German 200

40 Painted cloth St. Nicholas, missing robe and miter, wooden shoes; Dutch 150

41 Papier-mâché Father Christmas, long felt coat; German* 300–500

42 Papier-mâché Santa Claus, wire armature; German 55–60

43 Father Christmas with wooden face, fur-covered reindeer; probably German 1,200

44 Papier-mâché Father Christmas, flocked plaster reindeer; German 700–800

45 Plaster over papier-mâché Father Christmas, goose-feather tree; German 250

46 Father Christmas, Celluloid face, cotton-wadding suit; German 225–250

47 Plaster over papier-mâché Father Christmas, near fence; German* 450

48 Composition Santa Claus on snowball; German* 75–85

49 Santa Claus, scrap face, cotton-wadding body, snowballs; German* 225

50 Papier-mâché "scratching" Father Christmas; German 400–500

51 Papier-mâché Father Christmas; German 300

52 Santa jump-up in cardboard box; German 100

53 Papier-mâché Santa on log; German* 55–75

54 Papier-mâché Santa on logs; German* 55–75

55 Santa-in-a-sleigh, small; Danish 150

56 Papier-mâché Père Noël, cotton-wadding clothing; French 800

57 Left: bisque Santa Claus head ashtray; Japanese 200

Right: plaster Father Christmas tree light; German 400

58 Father Christmases, painted carved wood; Russian 200 each

59 Molded-cardboard Father Christmas; German 100–125

60 Composition Father Christmas-in-a-sleigh and reindeer, small; German 65–75

61 Papier-mâché Father Christmas, smiling, prominent teeth; German* 200

62 Painted formed-cardboard Father Christmas, "pointy" beard; German* 350

63 Papier-mâché Santa-on-skis; German 75

*Figure is a candy container.

**100**

| | | | |
|---|---|---|---|
| 64 | Bisque-faced Father Christmas, toy sack; German* | $ 250 | |
| 65 | Assorted "saucy" Father Christmas candy boxes; German/West German* | 20–30 | |
| | Foreground: Santa candy cornucopia, scrap face; German* | 35 | |
| 66 | Santa Claus, painted mask face, mitten hands; German | 300–400 | |
| 67 | Musical Santa Claus, painted mask face, mitten hands; German | 300–400 | |
| 68 | Santa Claus, painted mask face, mitten hands; German | 200 | |
| 69 | Santa Claus, painted mask face, mitten hands; German | 350–400 | |
| 70 | "Dishrag" Santa; probably American | 150 | |
| 71 | "Immobile Teeny" Santa on motorcycle; German | 55–65 | |
| 72 | Immobile Teeny Santa pushing cart of goodies; German | 70 | |
| 73 | Immobile Teeny Santa in car; German | 55 | |
| 74 | Left: Immobile Teeny Father Christmas with bad boy; German | 75 | |
| | Center: Immobile Teeny Father Christmas visiting child in bed; German | 65–75 | |
| | Right: Immobile Teeny Snowbaby in igloo, Father Christmas above; German | 85 | |
| 75 | La Befana; Italian | 1,000 | |
| 76 | Père Noël, mask face, cotton-wadding suit; French* | 600 | |
| 77 | Papier-mâché Santa Claus, short coat; German* | 175 | |
| 78 | Buster Brown formed-cardboard Santa; German | 80 | |
| 79 | Steiff Santa Claus with rubber face; German | 150–175 | |
| 80 | Ceramic Santa incense burner; German | 75 | |
| 81 | "Minerve" Santa, small; French | 30 | |
| 82 | Bisque Father Christmas, satin suit; probably Japanese* | 175 | |
| 83 | Left: papier-mâché Santa-in-sleigh; German | 50–75 | |
| | Right: Santa-in-a-sleigh, wax face; German | 100–150 | |
| 84 | Miniature Santa-in-a-sleigh, Celluloid; Japanese | 30 | |
| 85 | Santa-in-a-sleigh, clay face; Japanese | 45–55 | |
| 86 | "Aleut" Santa, clay face; Japanese | 50–60 | |
| 87 | Papier-mâché Santa-in-a-sleigh, reindeer; Japanese | 45–55 | |

| | | | |
|---|---|---|---|
| 88 | Santa Claus on candy box, cotton-wadding suit; Japanese* | $ 100–125 | |
| 89 | Basic Santa Claus figures; Japanese | 35–55 | |
| 90 | Santa Claus, clay face, all-chenille suit; Japanese | 75 | |
| 91 | Santa Claus, composition face, highly colored; Japanese | 75–100 | |
| 92 | Assorted pine cone Santas; Japanese | 10–25 | |
| 93 | Celluloid Father Christmas/Santa figures; American and Japanese | 20–35 | |
| 94 | Celluloid roly-poly Santa-on-a-ball; Japanese | 40 | |
| 95 | Celluloid Santa-on-a-train rattle; Japanese | 50–60 | |
| 96 | Celluloid and metal "rocker" Santa; Japanese | 55–65 | |
| 97 | Left: molded-glass Santa light bulb, small; Japanese | 50 | |
| | Right: molded-glass Santa light bulb, large; Japanese | 125–150 | |
| 98 | Cardboard church with Santa in front; Japanese* | 45–55 | |
| 99 | Cardboard house with clay Santa on patio; Japanese | 45–55 | |
| 100 | Santa riding in cardboard airship; Japanese* | 200–250 | |
| 101 | Santa riding in cardboard airplane; Japanese | 60 | |
| 102 | Chenille-covered Santa boot, to hang; Japanese* | 50–60 | |
| 103 | Foil-covered Santa boot, to hang; Japanese* | 50–60 | |
| 104 | Flannel boot with Celluloid Santa face; Japanese* | 50–60 | |
| 105 | Flannel and straw basket with Santa face; Japanese* | 50 | |
| 106 | Three net candy bags with Celluloid Santa faces; Japanese* | 45–65 | |
| 107 | Hanging Santa bell with clay face; Japanese | 50 | |
| 108 | Hanging Santa, chenille ropes; Japanese | 15 | |
| 109 | Hanging Santa candy bag, clay face; Japanese* | 30–45 | |
| 110 | A wreath of Santas | | |
| | 1 Japanese milk-glass light bulb | 25 | |
| | 2 German bisque torso Santa Claus | 45 | |

*Figure is a candy container.

3 American "Keepsake Egg" Santa head wearing glasses — $ 5

4 American Norman Rockwell Santa — 5

5–6 Japanese chenille Santas, clay faces, small — 5

7 American Santa with fabric hat — 5

8 German blown-glass Santa tree ornament, large — 60

9 Ecuadoran woven-straw Santa* — 6

10 Japanese milk-glass light bulb — 10–15

11 Japanese googly-eyed Santa with glass head — 4

12 German painted plaster Father Christmas — 25

13 American cardboard cutout Santa light bulb — 20

14 German painted lead Santa — 10–15

15 German painted plaster Father Christmas — 25

16 Japanese milk-glass light bulb — 10

17 Taiwanese plastic Father Christmas — 6

18 Japanese milk-glass light bulb — 10–15

19 Japanese bisque Santa — 15

20 Japanese cotton-wadding Santa torso, clay face — 30

21 Japanese two-sided milk-glass light bulb with Santa face — 10

22 Occupied Japan flannel-suited Santa — 35

23 American cookie Santa from St. Louis, Missouri — 20

24 Japanese bisque Santa on sled — 15

25 American early Hallmark stuffed-cotton Santa — 10

111 Pressed-cardboard Santa and fireplace scene; probably American* — 25

112 Four pressed-cardboard Santa figures; American* — 15–45

113 Pressed-glass Father Christmas candy container; American* — 75–100

114 Candy sack with chromolithographed Father Christmas; probably American* — 50

115 "Walk-man" Santa, composition and fabric; American — $ 60

116 Printed cardboard standup Santa with easel back; American — 40

117 Santa-in-a-sleigh, reindeer; U.S. Occupied Zone of Germany — 200–250

118 Santa jump-up in box, felt face; West German — 50–65

119 Papier-mâché Father Christmas; West German — 45

120 Santa pouring Coca-Cola, plastic face; American — 50–75

121 Santa promoting Longines watches; American — 35

122 Santa cooking at old Eagle Stove; American — 35

123 Stuffed cotton Santa; probably American — 35

124 Gnomelike Santa holding two children; probably American — 85–100

125 Santa cast-iron still bank; American — 90–100

126 Typical post–World War II Santa figures; Japanese — 15–25

127 Santa-in-a-chimney, tin, key windup; Japanese — 35

128 Santa-in-a-sleigh, reindeer, key windup; Japanese — 30–40

129 Santa-on-motorcycle, Celluloid, metal bell, key windup; Japanese — 25–35

130 "SuperSanta"; Japanese — 15

131 Battery-operated tin Santa, rings bell; American — 45

132 Santa on metal world globe, vinyl face; American — 50–75

133 Papier-mâché Father Christmas (*Babbo Natale*); Italian — 35–50

134 "Log" Santas, felt trimmed; Spanish — 8

135 Painted plastic Father Christmas, orlon suit; Austrian — 20

136 All-wool Santa from Lanz of Salzburg; Austrian — not for sale

137 Santa, carved wooden face and hands; Hungarian — 75–85

138 Santa, painted cotton-felt face, from Dresden; East German — 30

139 Lacquered tin Santa; Mexican — 20

140 Painted clay Santa; El Salvadoran — 30

141 *Jultomten*, Sculpey face and hands; Swedish — 35–65

142 *Jultomten*, vinyl face and hands, wool clothes; Swedish — 35–50

*Figure is a candy container.

143 *Jultomten*, painted, carved wood; Swedish $ 50–60

144 *Julnisse*, hemp and wood; Danish 30

145 Painted bisque Santa and Father Christmas figures; Taiwanese 10–35

146 Grandfather Frost, composition face, satin robe; Russian 250–300

147 Plastic Grandfather Frost, cotton-wadding robe; Russian 275

148 Painted plastic Grandfather Frost; Russian 75–100

149 Left: stuffed cotton-velvet Santa; American 40

Center: plastic troll Santa; probably American 35

Right: Steiff Santa, plastic face, metal glasses; West German 35

150 Santa, felt and cotton, mink trim;

American $ 50–75

151 Painted plaster Father Christmas under dome; American 75

152 Contemporary Father Christmas by Faith Wicks; American 375–400

153 Hygroscopic Father Christmas soap figure; Taiwanese and American 10

154 Lithographed tin Santa from Hallmark Cards, Inc.; American 20

155 Roly-poly Santa tobacco tin, Chein Industries; American 15

156 Contemporary carved wood Father Christmas; American 75

157 "Annalee" Santa, felt face, wire armature; American 350–400

158 Pine cone Father Christmas, plaster face, flax beard; American 400–450

159 Rear view of plate 158 showing toys in pack

160 Father Christmas, velvet suit, fur trim; American 250–300